SUCCESS BEYOND GAME DAY

THE PLAYBOOK TO LEVERAGE YOUR GRIT, WILL YOUR WAY TO GREATNESS, AND GO PRO IN LIFE

SUCCESS BEYOND GAME DAY

THE PLAYBOOK TO LEVERAGE YOUR GRIT, WILL YOUR WAY TO GREATNESS, AND GO PRO IN LIFE

SAMANTHA CARD

ethos
collective

SUCCESS BEYOND GAME DAY © 2024 by Samantha Card.
All rights reserved.

Printed in the United States of America

Published by Ethos Collective™
PO Box 43, Powell, OH 43065
www.ethoscollective.vip

This book contains material protected under international and federal copyright laws and treaties. Any unauthorized reprint or use of this material is prohibited. No part of this book may be reproduced or transmitted in any form or by any means, electronic or mechanical, including photocopying, recording, or by any information storage and retrieval system, without express written permission from the author.

LCCN: 2023924368
Paperback ISBN: 978-1-63680-253-4
Hardcover ISBN: 978-1-63680-254-1
e-book ISBN: 978-1-63680-255-8

Available in paperback, hardcover, e-book, and audiobook.

Any Internet addresses (websites, blogs, etc.) and telephone numbers printed in this book are offered as a resource. They are not intended in any way to be or imply an endorsement by Ethos Collective™, nor does Ethos Collective™ vouch for the content of these sites and numbers for the life of this book.

Some names and identifying details may have been changed to protect the privacy of individuals.

Opening Credits

In loving memory of Fred Harry who was an important mentor, leader, and accountability partner who helped me navigate what success beyond sports looked like for this Miami, Florida athlete.

To my family and close friends (you know who you are), you continue to provide the strong foundation, positive environment, and overall support to go ALL IN. Mom, you are my rock, my sounding board, my lighthouse, the real MVP! You are everything to me.

To my "guide on the side," Brittney Ezell. You have become such a spark and change agent for my personal and professional growth. You make me a better human. I am inspired by you. You have taught me how to take on life with the joyous intensity that you do. You have always seen, heard, and valued me. You are more than just a mentor and coach. You are my dear friend. You have a lifer in me.

And my dear friend, Caleb Campbell. There are not enough words to highlight your importance in my life. I admire you. I respect you. I see you. You have helped me feel my heart in a way I didn't think was possible beyond sports. You enhanced my capacity to be present in the now. You always root for me and just know, I am forever grateful for the soul you are and continue to be.

*Excellence is not a singular act but a habit.
You are what you repeatedly do.*

—Shaquille O'Neal

Table of Contents

Foreword ix

Chapter 1: Winner Mentality 101 1

Chapter 2: From Your Limelight Moment to "In Your Feelings" 13

Chapter 3: Setback to the Comeback 26

Chapter 4: Your Athlete Advantage 41

Chapter 5: Your Post-Sports Afterglow 57

Chapter 6: On and Off the Field: Go Time 73

Chapter 7: Athletes Are THE Best Bet, Period 88

Chapter 8: The $10 Billion Project in 5 Weeks 109

Chapter 9: Championship Routine in Place 121

Chapter 10: Being an Athlete Is a Business 142

Chapter 11: Higher Highs and Higher Lows 164

Chapter 12: Raise the Bar: Elevation Requires Separation 176

Endnotes 187

About the Author 189

Foreword

I still remember my first call with Samantha. A mutual friend of ours, Brittney Ezell, told me she had a friend I had to meet—no questions asked. And 30 seconds into the call, I immediately understood why.

Samantha is easily one of the most expansive people I've ever met. Meaning, it's impossible to be in her presence, personally or virtually, and not feel the possibility of what life can be. No, seriously. You think you have a vision for your life, and then you meet Samantha.

The heart-infused wisdom and unmatched energy that she leads with wipes away the smallness from your vision while empowering you with the tools needed to step into the fullness of who you are—individually and collectively.

And while I'm so grateful for the work that she is sharing with the world, what I love the most about her is the heart behind the work.

I'm a strong believer that, as leaders, we can't lead people where we aren't willing to go ourselves. And in today's world, it's easy to talk about authenticity, vulnerability, and inner growth. But to live it—to say yes to the fire of transformation—takes courage. And, as I've had a chance to deepen my relationship with Samantha, it has become increasingly clear that she embodies these values in every aspect of her life.

Her willingness to embrace her own journey of transformation, with all its trials and triumphs, makes her not just a leader but a beacon for those seeking to find their own path to personal and collective fulfillment. Samantha is

Foreword

a living example that true leadership comes from a place of deep self-awareness and a commitment to personal growth, and I know that her work will impact you as much as it has me.

—Caleb Campbell West Point Graduate | Army Lieutenant | Former NFL Linebacker | Keynote Speaker – Well-Being, Resilience, Mindset, and Mental Health

1

Winner Mentality 101

There is no "I" in TEAM, but there is an "M" and an "E"...

Practice doesn't make perfect. Practice makes permanence.
—Coach Larry Gelwix

You made it! You are officially a part of something bigger than you ever imagined. We are about to have some real fun, and it is ALL UP TO YOU! No family, friends, teammates, or business partners to hide behind. This is Day 1. Imagine the first time you felt full-fledged passion for the sport you played your whole life. For me, it was six years old. Nothing else mattered, and it was fun! Then, slowly but surely, it started to become a mission and ultimately a job to get to the highest level. Our journey together will be all about elevation, breaking down barriers, and exploring YOU, the brand. We will have focused attention on learning, leveraging, leveling up, and building your life legacy beyond sports. If the thought of this doesn't fire you up, I am not too sure what will. It's level-up season, my friend! Put up or shut up!

Before we get to work, let's address what you may be thinking: **"Who the heck is Sam Card?" "Why is she qualified?" "Is she another chick trying to pave her way?" "And why should I listen?"** I hear you, and I take your challenge.

I wouldn't be here if I didn't have No. 1 oozing out of me. Yes, my accolades will speak for themselves, but what makes me your differentiator is my transparency, bridge building, and open-book nature that knows how to get you where you want to go. I don't tell you what you want to hear. I am addressing what you need to hear, even if others have been too afraid to breach the topics.

I can just hear you thinking, "I know others who are open and transparent. I'm not sold yet on Sam Card." My response: "But do the others give you the full recipe?" I highlight and discuss where I've failed just as much as where I've excelled. I give you the full view, not a piece of it. And the most important aspect of all is that I want you to be better than me, in all ways. How many times do you hear that from others, let alone believe it? Well, here I am, needing nothing from you but your effort and character. I am willing to serve you with information that can be your reason why your first door opens post-sports. I want you to leverage me and my network to succeed beyond the game, period! I am not looking to advertise who I've helped, but rather let your growth and success be what feeds my urge to give back 10x over. So, on to my accolades because I know you need to see that before you read on.

Since every day is an interview, I will take the bait. I was formally known as "Sammi from Miami," a former NCAA Division I softball player at the University of Pittsburgh. I graduated in 2009 (during the 2009 market collapse) with a Bachelor of Science degree in chemistry. From undergrad, I went straight into getting my Master of Business Administration (MBA) in 2010, focused on strategy and marketing. Like many of you, sports were my life, and I didn't get to participate in internships or work while playing. In essence, I started my Day 1 post-sports with ZERO years of work experience (more to come on this). I studied abroad in Marseille, France, for half a year to gain more international exposure at 24 years old. I pride myself on taking on the uncomfortable and at times the "not possible" endeavors.

Winner Mentality 101

During the last month of my MBA, I was recruited by a Fortune 100 company headhunter for a marketing analyst position, just 27 days before I graduated in 2012. I graduated on a Friday and started work on Monday, with my first week on the job in Doha, Qatar, in the Middle East. At this point in my life, I may have had 10 stamps in my passport. Talk about getting uncomfortable and persevering—95% of my job interviews had been over the phone, and I only met my boss in person at the airport in D.C. headed to Qatar, no joke! Please remember this was only Week 1 of my corporate career—no big deal! Straight grow through what you go through.

Beyond having zero years of "traditional" work experience right out of sports, I also had never (and still haven't to this day) been in a role that existed before. Just think, no one came before me, but I helped build the role out, make it my own, to ultimately, one day, hand it off to someone else to make it their own. This right here is as rare as it gets in corporate America! To give you a view, from Week 1 forward, think: sprint throughout the marathon, drink from the fire hydrant, leverage my game day skills to slow the game down, stay uncomfortable, mitigate language barriers, and challenge conservative traditions to drive step change growth while embracing a legacy that was foundationally strong. Easy, right? Ha! I always knew I could leverage my athletic building blocks to figure out the ambiguity and create limitless possibilities! I was showing results, first in and last out every day, and then I was fortunate to be put through the Marketing Best Bet program with the chief marketing officer and vice presidents in the organization, which further advertised my brand.

In Year 2, I led a team to create the first farmer sulfur nutrition return-on-investment calculator in the company. Agriculture in the USA is critically important to our economy, so you can imagine how exciting it was to be a part of the industry that feeds the world! Anything new and helping others see value on their returns versus their investments was my thing! My major career intersection came at the tail end of Year 2 and into Year 3 when I got tapped on the shoulder to help drive a $10B merger and acquisition assignment in five weeks. With a team of six, we achieved major success, and it further solidified my position up the executive track and into the succession plan at 26 years old.

At the height of it all, I helped my business group executive leader revitalize our five-year strategy and serve as her right hand. This leader was always destined for greatness, and I am convinced that this and her integration assignment further solidified her future as the CEO of the spinoff of the Fortune 100 company. As the spinoff was announced, I quickly realized I was "protected," "ring fenced," and "locked in a contract with no exit strategy" to go with the business and help drive the success into its own publicly traded company. Even though I do not like being told I don't have an option, it is important to see the silver lining in all things.

Thus, my next adventure came with yet another rare opportunity to help create my next role, Global Product Manager of a +$100M portfolio. I wanted to be accountable for a P&L (profit and loss) and hone my business financial acumen. I was obsessed with learning about the structure of balance sheets and income statements, driving new product introductions, managing mix product, changing how the culture of a legacy organization views quality, and growing the P&L by millions of dollars year after year. As we spun off, I was fortunate to lead the enterprise marketing transition team, going into the spinoff in 2016. Meaning, we built from the ground up all things branding, logos, and colors, creating a corporate site in three weeks, consolidating a domain, and taking our first steps toward creating our new identity outside of the big fortune 100 behemoth.

Roll forward to 2021, and I have grown my corporate portfolio significantly (eight figures, aka multi millions to be exact) and made great strides in building my personal wealth legacy. To be clear, in order to achieve wealth (not rich status), you will need to acquire assets and have those assets make you more money while you sleep. It was a rude awakening to discover that I needed more than a corporate paycheck each month to create wealth. You need a championship routine in place to align and structure what is important to you and why. We will dig into this later in the book.

Since graduation, I have had the honor to formally and informally mentor athletes of all backgrounds while growing my own brand in parallel. Helping other athletes is an honor and major passion of mine. It really clicked when a former athlete asked, "Why don't you do this full-time?" What a moment in 2020! That one conversation changed me and my career trajectory. Let that sink in. One conversation, one, YES. One percent better every day is all it takes sometimes. So, yes, every day is an interview!

I am here to lay out the playbook I will continue to utilize, so you can leverage what I have done well and build upon that, as well as learn from where I've failed or tolerated problems. I am passionate about your success post-sports, so much so that I left corporate America and a six-figure career to dedicate my life from here on out to help athletes like you succeed beyond game day! There is no ulterior motive, just mere respect for having been in your shoes as a former athlete and the desire to help you take it up a notch! I am so humbled by your trust in me to help you. We will be navigating through my consolidated learnings and inspiration from athletics to life post-sports into corporate trailblazing. Let's get into it!

So, now that you know who I am and what I am about, let's get back to it! We are a TEAM, but it's about YOU and how you can LEVERAGE and raise the bar for yourself and others around you. Do you have it in you to get uncomfortable about where you really are as an individual and a brand? What does life post-sports look like to you?

Let's peel back the onion, explore your layers, and find what the championship routine looks like for you. Remember, how you do anything is how you do everything. I challenge you to pause and reflect on the below questions, as we will use these throughout the book.

1. Who are you outside of being an athlete? (Many athletes feel a black hole post-graduation.)

2. Many athletes, like yourself, are accustomed to the limelight, and when you graduate, are you confident of your next steps? (Don't give me something fake here. Be honest with where base is!)

3. What happens if you don't make it pro in your sport? (This is a counterintuitive winner mentality approach—your exit strategy, aka plan B. Don't worry; we will dig into this!)

4. How can you successfully transition from being a top 1% performer to finding real-world career success? (One percent better every darn day.)

5. Will you ever find that passion outside of being an athlete like you felt during game day? (This is a tough one that many struggle with—just think, it took me 12 years.)

6. Do you know anything as much as you know sports? (I didn't for a while.)

7. Now that you can be paid for your brand and likeness, how do you know a good deal from a bad one? (Equity versus a check every time—Chapter 10 hits on this.)

8. How do you manage relationships while you are building up your championship routine? (We will dive into "closing the gap"—one of the harder concepts once you hit success, or it might even prevent you from achieving ultimate success.)

Now you may be reading the above questions and feel unprepared, still unsure of what major interests you have, behind the curve, or even overwhelmed. This is normal! I want you to feel this! In some cases, you may feel anxious. Remember, we are elite athletes who know how to WIN. The great thing about you is that you are competitive, coachable, and resilient. You know how to prepare, stay disciplined, and set a championship routine already! All I am doing is helping to guide you to leverage these skills gained over your sports career and apply them in different ways!

Let's dig into why you started sports in the first place. Some may say it was your escape from the chaos or bad crowds, a way out of your hometown, aka the "bubble," to be the first in your family to make it through college, to get a free education, or even just to feel the Friday Night Lights. No matter what your reason is, we all have a "WHY," and from that comes the start of the highest form of your current self. What I mean is, you worked hard to get your physical and mental self into shape at a young age so you could make it to game day. You waited (or are waiting) for the college letters, phone calls, scouting tournaments, videos online for coaches, and so much more. Many athletes have their hands up and work hard, but guess what? The coaches picked you! In those moments you realize all the extra practice, zero vacations/time off, and lack of social life were all worth it. This is where the elite get built.

My reason was the competition and challenge. I was obsessed with achieving elite status. It was not about having the best swing, but rather a deep-down desire to enable a whole team to shift gears and find a way to win. I wanted to play with and against the "best of the best" at all times! I always tried to play above my age growing up. When I was 12, I wanted to play with the 16- to 18-year-old players. I never wanted the game to slow down because that meant I was too comfortable when all I wanted to do was compete with the best of the best. To give you a good sense, I used to fly out all over the country to play for a team based in another state with a bunch of A players. This team had players go to the University of Pittsburgh (H2P!), University of Alabama, University of Michigan, Stanford, University of Florida, Mississippi State, Virginia Tech, University of Arizona, James Madison University, and the list goes on! Many are still close friends today. It is an understatement that your teammates become family that you choose.

My life was sports. My mission and goal were to set up a championship routine and prepare to play Division I sports. Just like you, I would play year-round, no work internship opportunities or spring/summer vacations. You learn to sacrifice early on because sports is life, period! Whether you're always winning or on an underdog team, there is the "winner mentality" that is hard to explain to those who do not have it. It lives in an athlete, and you tap into this "beast mode" that most people will never tap into. Think, failure is not an option or consideration.

> You already know how to set up a championship routine, so let's break it down.

1. Tap into your innate belief and deep-rooted will to WIN.
2. Assess what stands in your way by eliminating problems, not tolerating them.
3. Leverage skill sets you have acquired from an early age.
4. Build new skills and leverage other teammates' skill sets.
5. Lay the foundation and groundwork strategies through practice, film, lifting, and nutrition.
6. Play to WIN every day, every game, and every chance you get.

THIS IS YOUR ATHLETE ADVANTAGE!

You already know how to win in sports, and I am here to "level you up" in all aspects of life by showing you how to identify opportunities, take action, and apply the life tools gained in competitive sports to business success. We will not only get you in the right rooms but also prepare you for how best to navigate those rooms and drive your brand! I will say this often: You are the brand!

Success Beyond Game Day Playbook is based upon five key components, which I acquired through my experiences in sports, in corporate America, and with immense inspiration from Ray Dalio's Principles[1] **and Dr. Steve L. Robbins' What If.**[2] I have integrated a lot of thought-provoking lessons learned from their books and in person and have applied them to my daily life while also incorporating new layers as I learn and progress. For the remainder of the book, the playbook below will be integrated in every chapter and chapter play-by-play snapshots.

Success Beyond Game Day Playbook

> **Don't blame, fail fast, take the quick learning, blueprint, implement, and repeat.**
>
> 1. **Go beyond setting goals** on Day 1. Write them down, print them out, sign them, and look at them every day. Be obsessed and measurable. This is a contract with yourself.
>
> 2. **Identify the problem. Do not tolerate problems**, aka red flags.
>
> 3. **Peel back the layers**, go below the surface, and ask yourself the "six whys" (See Chapter 11) every time. Be disciplined with this.
>
> 4. **Lay the groundwork and foundation** with optionality and levers.
>
> 5. **Flawless operationalization**. It's game time! Commit and be about it!

When the clock is ticking down, are you the one making the shot? You better have said yes! Get ready to learn, stretch yourself, and be humble because it will serve you well when getting into the most important rooms in the future.

What happens when your championship routine takes a personal pride setback? Maybe you didn't get the "yes" or have the followers or popularity you expected, or even worse, you have others voting on your performance. We all know they have only seen the surface level, and their judgments are primarily based on stats and marketability factors. Ah! This still irks me to this day. Like you, I know what it takes to work your tail off to be the best of the best. It becomes deflating when it comes down to one person's "decision," or a group of individuals (who may or may not have ever played the sport they are judging you on) that determines if you get your accolade. Surface-level thoughts with minimal substance and a whole lot of politics drive many decisions in this world. You must deal with the punches. I am a competitor! If you beat me straight up, I will be the first to spread the roses, but what happens if something doesn't go your way even though you earned it? Let's explore this!

2

From Your Limelight Moment to "In Your Feelings"

Think about where you are today as a high-performing athlete. You can be in college, the NFL, NHL, MLB, WNBA, NBA, Olympics, any other professional capacity, or transitioning to the next level. Is the game slowing down yet? Or are you still drinking from the fire hydrant? Are you at your new Day 1? Have you had more 150% effort days or more "off," 90% days?

No matter what stage in your athletic life cycle you are at, I am confident you know what a "W" feels like just as much as you know what an "L" feels like. You know the difference between a morning, afternoon, or night game; they feel different. You know the rush of adrenaline that overcomes you while playing in front of a loud crowd or right before heading out to the big game. That amped feeling you get where your heart starts beating out of your chest, and you suddenly get an eerie calm all over your body, knowing you have home field advantage. Or the feeling in the pit in your stomach when you are in unfamiliar territory, the weather conditions playing against you, while fans translate their passion for the sport into "Your mom doesn't even love you" chants, and upon your look over your shoulder, they now know you hear them.

From Your Limelight Moment to "In Your Feelings"

I still remember an away game, playing Notre Dame, and one of our fans belted out, "Rudy was offsides. I hope the umps aren't as bad as the refs you had back in the day on the football field!" This got a rise out of everyone, including the Notre Dame coaches. Sports drives passion, excitement, and a deep-rooted feeling of escape and promise for all involved. As athletes, we are fortunate to put a show on for the crowd. The same applies to real life post-sports! As many say, "I am married to the game." For many of us, it is who we are! All we know!

Now think about a point in life where you felt at least one personal or physical setback. Did it take you away from your sport? How long did it last? Did you feel resentment, or did you crush the walls closing in on you? Did it involve family, friends, teammates, and/or relationships? Was it something you could control? Were those around you helpful or distracting? Did someone not hold their end up of a bargain? Did you hold your own weight?

Picture your breakout year, with the game slowed down, having complete control over how and what you respond to, and every play in the game clear as day. If you haven't experienced it yet, a great way to understand this is remembering your first time driving by yourself. When you were 16 years old, your first time in the car without supervision, you were hyper-aware of everything. You wanted to change the volume without taking your hands off the wheel, stopped six feet before the white line at a red light, stuck to the speed limit (exact number), looked in your rearview mirror, anxious about someone tailgating (about to beep), and had a red-knuckle-tight grip on your wheel (always two hands on the wheel). In some cases, your anxiousness overcame you, and you completely forgot what a traffic sign meant, but you internally reminded yourself that you passed the driver's test.

Success Beyond Game Day

After you got your "cool" out of the way, wasted a tank of gas, and came home, do you remember how tired you were? I do. I took a nap! You were operating on all cylinders, processing all your surroundings. Think of this as your freshman year, Day 1. Look how you drive now. It is second nature to drive with one hand on the wheel, let your experiences help you anticipate. You process faster and are proactive, less reactive to your circumstances. This is a good way to think of "slowing the game down." You see the situation play out before it occurs. You can strategically navigate the situation pending the outcome desired. Slowing the game down to a point where it feels like "the matrix" is a different type of superpower and major athlete advantage because we spend our whole careers mastering this each day.

My breakout year was junior year at Pitt. I remember that whole season from fall ball to spring season. Of course, I trained hard like you would, but it felt different. I transitioned from practicing hitting peas with a stick for hand-eye coordination to hitting dry rice grains while catching a tennis ball being thrown at me at the same time. The game slowed down. I was able to take on a harder workload, on top of my chemistry major workload. During this season I took inorganic, analytical, calculus 3, and p-chem on top of an anticipated heavy travel schedule. I was a co-captain, a responsibility that I took seriously. I had to be at 150% well over 99% of the time, and for that 1% "off day," I had to be at 98%. I needed to get 1% better every day. I had to set the pace and tone on and off the field. I was not going to let someone outwork me, period.

Let me give you a feel for how my junior year fall ball set the tone. I was just at the tail end of mono (two weeks). I was weak, having lost about 10 pounds, but I didn't care. I wanted to play. It was the only time period at Pitt that I was told I would be sitting out before the game. I was "in my feelings"

From Your Limelight Moment to "In Your Feelings"

and emotional, but remember, as a captain, I had a bigger role than my personal pride. All I knew was if an opportunity presented itself, I was going to be ready!

It was the bottom of the seventh inning, two outs, runner on second, and we were down by two runs. In that moment, my coach looked at me—no words, just a look, asking without asking. I nodded and got my helmet and bat, stood at the front of the dugout, and waited for the official call. Next thing you know, I was up to bat. My philosophy was always "aggressive, early attack and go 100% all-in on the best pitch." Understand that I did not warm up, did not play the whole game, but when the time came to make something happen, I was chosen. Since I was not 100% physically, my goal was to hit the ball hard to the right side, knock in the runner from second, and just make it to first base. I would not leave first base until someone healthier was able to come in and run for me. What happened? Exactly that! I didn't care how good it looked, I was razor-focused on making it happen, changing the momentum of the game, and getting the run in. We won! Mind over matter wins every single time!

Yes, it was an offseason game, but as mentioned before, the offseason is where champions and championships are made. This intention set the tone for the season ahead. No excuses, just results! As I entered the season, I performed well, stayed consistent, but we still lost too many games! The best part of the season was when I hit my peak in the postseason during conference play. I was batting over .444. I also managed to be a three- and four-hitter who stole a lot of bases. I was by no means the fastest one on the team, but I sure knew how to read situations. I was a catcher who had the privilege to call the games. The coaches had faith in me to see and navigate the field of play. I leveraged the game, slowing down to capitalize on finding those opportunities. I did not have to wait for my coaches to tell me but rather felt enabled to take ownership of the outcomes in a bigger way. **A big lesson that I still utilize today in corporate America is that you should enable people to make decisions and take ownership! You will hear me say this multiple times: Work smarter, not harder!**

I want to give you a chance to see what I saw when I would step into the batter's box. I assessed the mannerism of the pitcher and catcher as I set myself up in the front of the batter's box. I knew what pitches were coming based off small tells, grips, quirks, and eye contact. I had my metal cleats fully gripping into the clay, a light grip on the bat, eerily calm, ready to go at the first opportunity and unleash. The batter's box was about 40 feet away, so hand-eye coordination was the name of the game. I was at a point in my career where I was able to see the spin of the ball in slow motion while only having a fraction of a second to react. Standing in the front of the box gave myself less time. I had to attack before the pitch broke, which in turn gave me more of a chance to hit based off my game plan: straight proactive offense.

From Your Limelight Moment to "In Your Feelings"

Your intention and outcome can proportionally change when you are prepared and stick to your game plan. Think about it like this: In softball, the ball trajectory can go up, in, out, and down, whereas in baseball, it can go down, in, and out. It is the major difference between underhand and overhand pitching. The unknown and speed is greater in softball, in my humble opinion. Happy to take you out and show you one of these days when I visit your school!

As athletes, we set our intention and obsess until we reach our goals. By the time we hit our goals, we already have a new and improved goal set to show that we are a consistent force to be reckoned with. We don't train to win once; we target repeating. By the end of my junior season, post-playoffs, I felt great personally but still wanted to win more games! I was fortunate to receive conference first-team honors and was in the running for Player of the Year. I had a few of the conference corporate leaders express their admiration for my postseason play.

For me, I was coming into my own as an elite athlete. I felt the game was right where it needed to be. I spent long nights struggling over the hard science curriculum, 8:00 p.m. labs worth one credit (a lot of work for one credit!), and studying in between lifting, practice, and recovery. To the athletic world, I was the "nerd," and to the academic world, I was a "jock." For the first time, I felt that I crystallized real results that had far-reaching impacts across the board. I was a scholar-athlete, and every bit of me tried to be elite in both.

After I was named first-team all-conference (joined by a few other teammates), the room got quiet for the Big East Player of the Year Award. I knew I had a good year, but it was not until I had other teams, coaches, and conference executives directly reach out and say you may take it during dinner that I thought it could be me! Me? I was just playing ball, focused on the "W," and working to get better each day. The

Success Beyond Game Day

Commissioner and Vice Chair of the Big East came up and began to lay out the introduction for the upcoming Player of the Year, and a lot of the stats (over 15 homeruns in pre/post season, double digit RBI's, over a 0.700 slugging percentage, and leading doubles in the conference) seemed like mine, but then I heard: "…first time we have a two-year-in-a-row winner, so it is history when I…" I literally didn't hear another word. For a split second, when I thought I was taking home "Player of the Year," my palms started sweating, and my heart rate picked up. I saw victory and got myself so disappointed when I didn't win.

Why am I sharing this? How does this help you succeed beyond game day?

Success during and beyond game day starts when you do not let moments like Player of the Year dictate who you are and how you move. It may feel like a bad day, but it isn't a bad life. You have a responsibility under the limelight, while everyone is watching, to show your true character. Listen, you should be upset you didn't win. Being second place doesn't feel great, and you should not be comfortable with just aiming for a medal. I am stressing that you have others looking for your reaction, hoping you have your 1% "off day" after this personal setback. Stay true to you and your purpose, always! Go back to the drawing board and add and make changes to get you to No. 1! In these moments when you don't get first place, look around and get a temperature reading around you. You learn more from failures than success.

In times of setback and adversity, let this fuel you in a positive way. Show others your character and poise. My idea of character is YOU DON'T IMPULSIVELY REACT, but rather have the courage to shake the winner's hand, give the other competitor their three-second roses, reflect, and get back to work the next day. That is character in its purest form!

From Your Limelight Moment to "In Your Feelings"

Look at Tom Brady and his work ethic. He is the G.O.A.T. because he put in the work, modified the game plan when needed, and showed up every day. Even with all the Super Bowl wins, many wanted to get their two minutes of fame on TV by doubting the champ! What did he do? He won another Super Bowl and had fun doing it! Same story for sprinter Allyson Felix, the champ, the Olympian (what a role model). She earned her place, created her own runway, adapted to change, embodied resiliency, and continued to win even after many didn't think she could last after 10-plus years of her sports career and the birth of her child. She is not only the G.O.A.T. in her sport, but she literally went head-to-head with Nike (parted ways), created her own brand, and wore her own brand shoe, Saysh Spike One, in the 2021 Tokyo Games, which solidified her becoming the most decorated athlete in track and field history. Heavy reminder: Check the temperature of the room when you win, when circumstances change, and when you lose. I guarantee you won't find the exact people in both rooms.

When you are at the top, many will try to tear you down. When you aren't first, many will make decisions on your "stock" worth to them—literally quantifying you as a person based on how much value you bring to the table. We can debate this, but I stand behind my belief that athletes are sensitive and emotional. We just harness our response on the field. We let our actions speak, not words. We feel hurt when others downgrade our stock value in public when they have never met us in person. It is life and part of the game. Being an athlete is a business, and every day is a negotiation; you must deal or be dealt a hand you didn't sign up for.

Think about it: Why do pro athletes get sensitive when they see a bad rating of them in a simple video game? Maybe it has a little to do with pride, but deep down it is because they aren't considered as valuable as someone else based on only "stock" value. I haven't been around anyone who likes to be the one picked last. People have a yearning to be included—maybe not liked, but they definitely want to be in the room.

A personal setback, in whatever form it comes in, humbles you, but it doesn't cripple you. No one is going to feel bad for you and give you a pass. Everyone is more focused on how you will respond to it. In every sport and corporate career, recruiters look for the bandwidth of all things you. Physicality and raw talent are why many athletes think they get chosen while being recruited, but in reality, it comes down to who they are (character) and what they embody (consistency and discipline). **Your raw talent is a big part of the decision of how you fit into a system, but your character, coachability, and how you respond to setbacks differentiate you from the pack in the program.** This right here is one of the areas where you can utilize being an athlete to succeed at the highest levels of business and corporate America!

Sample Questions Used in Interviews (some asked directly or indirectly):

1. *Tell me a little about yourself. Do you have experience with major successes and failures?*
2. *Tell me about a time when something didn't go the way you planned. What happened? How did you overcome it? How would have you improved the situation?*
3. *What are your "go to" tools, and how do you use them when a project has a tight timetable and with a team that doesn't see eye to eye?*
4. *What is important to you when choosing a role or company?*

5. *What differentiates you? What unique qualities have you used to lead? Why?*

Notice how they are less about the inherent physical skill sets needed for the job at hand and more around how you handle situations, your character, and your ability to handle adversity. Does that sound like many scenarios you have embarked on as an athlete already? Sports and business intersect in many ways, and guess what? You have many years of experience! Sometimes there will be critical skill sets required if a role is specialized, but for the most part, the above questions get asked. I have always struggled with how human resources function in corporate America. In many ways, they are in place to protect their companies, but they are supposed to be HUMAN resources within a corporation.

I have learned how to work with this function, establish the sandbox to work within, and leverage their expertise when needed. Every person and function has a place, so learn where they fit in your toolbox. But always know, if you build bridges, genuinely care about people, and listen to hear, not listen to respond, you will be good to go! People are what make corporations great; without them, you have nothing, so always be people first! Think beyond bell curves and end-of-the-year performance reports! Let those be a tool, but not an end-all, be-all! Let your actions and results speak!

As you begin to understand how much of what you learn in sports is applicable in the real world, the more you will realize how many gems you already have in your toolbox. There is a delicate balance between adding tools and leveraging the tools you innately have or have acquired over the years. Don't always resort to adding tools every time, but rather pause and assess the strong versatile tools you have at your disposal already. In other words, don't forget what you're great at when going after anything new. With new tools comes new skills (which is great), but sometimes you just need a bolt on to the tools (aka critical skill sets) you already possess. Work smarter, not harder!

Failures truly lead to the greatest breakthroughs. I am a living example of this! You will see the journey that got me to where I am today: the setbacks, character evolution, and winner mentality that has carried me throughout my journey. Learn from the failure by feeling "all the feels" first. When you welcome and acknowledge failure, especially when you are a born winner, the game changes. The way you approach the comeback becomes way more intentional and purpose-forward.

> **Two key sayings that I live by are (a little rough around the edges)**
>
> 1. **"PROPER PLANNING PREVENTS PISS POOR PERFORMANCE"**
> 2. **"BE INTENTIONAL, NOT RECREATIONAL"**

Set your game plan, react to the effectiveness, challenge yourself to be malleable when your outcome isn't what you planned for, see where the plan can be sharper, create a stronger foundation, and implement the new plan/program/system. Be intentional going forward. This is not a recreational sport, but rather a part of who you are. Set the plan in place and add measurable aspects to your goals to keep track. **A goal has a start and end date. If it does not, all you have is a dream, not a goal. Set an expiration date, or you will always remain where you started. Sign it! You no longer just have goals, but rather a binding contract with yourself. You** are only as good as your word and actions, so this is your most important contract in your life.

Be about it! Be the one called on with one second on the clock every time!

Success Beyond Game Day Playbook Recap:

From Your Limelight Moment to "In Your Feelings"

1. **Go beyond setting goals** on Day 1. Sign them, and now you have a contract.
   a. Make them SMART (specific, measurable, achievable, realistic, and time-bound).
   b. Focus on how you can WIN professionally and personally.
   c. Set aggressive timelines; never be outworked.
   d. Understand the difference between pivoting and improving your goals versus never meeting your goals end-to-end and just adding new ones.
   e. If you do not set timelines, your goals are just mere dreams.

2. **Identify the problem. Do not tolerate problems**, aka red flags.
   a. Don't equate an accolade with your overall success; it may validate what you are doing, but it does not define it.
   b. Be careful when making decisions. Do not respond when you are too emotional. A level head is always best, so take a breather.
   c. Take the "L," but NEVER be accustomed to being second best. Get back to work the NEXT DAY.

d. Check the pulse of the room when you win, change direction, or lose. Look for consistent presence from others around you. If not, have the courage to move on.

3. **Peel back the layers** and go below the surface. Ask yourself the six whys.
   a. Are you fighting your deep-down need to be validated by others? (It's you versus you).
   b. Are you afraid to start because you may fail in the future? Failure is the best lesson. (You will always be where you started if you do not take the first step. What is the worst thing that will happen? You fail? Get a NO? Are embarrassed? LEAVE YOUR EGO AND PRIDE AT THE DOOR—HUMBLE PIE SEASON IS UPON US).
   c. Afraid to go from HERO to ZERO if you lose your winner status? (Will repeat for those in the back, YOU versus YOU!)

4. **Lay the groundwork and foundation** with optionality and flexibility.
   a. Don't rebuild from the ground up when you get second; rather assess where you need to add more tools to improve and enhance on skills you already have.
   b. Do not lose track of what you do well when adding tools. Do not reinvent the wheel.
   c. If something works, do not change it, leverage it!

5. **Flawless operationalization**. Game time!

3

Setback to the Comeback

That Time I Broke My Spine in the Offseason… But Didn't

*Challenge yourself, go for it whatever "it" may be;
we are much more powerful and capable
than we will ever know.*

—Amy Purdy

The year after your breakout year is such a fascinating time. There's the cross between working harder than ever before and displaying your repeat elite place in the conversation. The inner beast mode is saying, "How much further can you raise the bar?" And your winner mentality is oozing out, giving you that extra confidence to handle the ones in the back of the room who are waiting to see if you are worth the conversation. Those types of people are the ones you have to entertain and just know, they won't go out of their way for you! But once you translate your "stock worth" and get them interested, they become your best leverage!

The constant question you will have to overcome is "Are you the truth or a fad?" For a long while after my junior season, I felt that I always had something to prove to everyone else. I never reflected on why I was painstakingly obsessed with impressing others until late in my senior year. Think about it: In life, why do we go out of our way to look, talk, and act a certain way to a group of people who don't know us? Does your inner desire to be included in the room drive your approach and ultimately "quench your thirst"? What do you do if you are thrown to the side because your "stock worth" was not positioned right? Or worse, because someone else made you believe they were championing your best interest, but translated your brand the wrong way? Remember, your network is your net worth, so be careful how you position yourself and who you allow in your inner circle (more on this later on).

The honest truth is that no one cares if you lost an award or had a personal setback. It really is you versus you. You may think people care, but they don't! Only you can determine how you respond to adversity, deciding what matters and where you go from there. In these moments where you go for it, and you are not well received or you have a setback, don't let your pride lead the charge. Best advice I have for you: Never make decisions when you are mad, sad, or extremely happy. Be levelheaded and check your emotions. Try to call yourself out when your feelings drive an impulse behavior. This applies to all aspects of your day-to-day such as a relationship, a missed pass, a dropped ball, a failed test, getting yelled at or disrespected by others. Rip the Band-Aid off, "feel all the feels," and move forward; do not tolerate a problem. If you do not have the headspace for the situation at hand, breathe, walk away, come back with a clear head, and course correct.

For example, have you ever been in practice, and a teammate fumbles an important play and then out of nowhere proceeds to blame you for the miss with a straight face? Whether or not it was true, he/she pointed the finger at you, in front of everyone, and deflected the issue. Now you need to deal with this (avoidance isn't the answer), and you deep-down know many others would get fired up. I get it! I challenge you in this situation to take a breath, say it won't happen again (in the current moment), and then after practice is over, go take them to lunch and talk through it. Same set of actions if you were on a business team in corporate America. You learn a lot more about the "why" and "what" that caused it when the environment is not highly charged with emotion.

Same would apply for a personal relationship when someone close lets you down. Don't react on your impulse. Check yourself, "walk away," and come back levelheaded to understand the WHY. Don't always lead with trying to solve the problem or start with stating your perspective; change it up and ask them what drove the situation. This is an area where I could have been better earlier on, but hey, I am human (and full of passion and will)! I focus on my headspace daily. I practice leading with intention and have accountability to my how, why, and when I react.

Roll forward to my senior year, you know the drill, the fall offseason prepping for our spring start. The team tries new rotations, "game-like" practice, except for the pitchers or red jersey QBs (aka the "princess" positions in any sport), and establishes the pace for the upcoming season. The offseason is when the freshman adapts to the new program, learns the difference between kilograms and pounds in the weight room, or falls because they have never worn metal cleats before. One of my favorites is when one of the newbies would throw up during conditioning (rookie things), and as you know, the list goes on. But the offseason is truly where you can get 1% better every day without being under the microscope from the outside world. You can truly insulate, set your pace, enlist extra help in areas of your game, and take the time to do it over and over until you get it right. I know you all know that the offseason is where champions are made. I truly believe that! It is when no one is looking, where the real transformation and overcoming failure after failure after failure becomes who you are and how you roll. You don't always want to do it, especially when everyone is partying on vacation, but those who stick to the plan with discipline and consistency every day are the elite!

As athletes, when we compete, we compete, period. Halfway is not in our DNA. It doesn't matter if we are playing a pickup game of basketball, racing someone outside, playing flag football, doing a lifting circuit, or playing a warmup game, we go 150%. We are born full-throttle winners because we know the feeling of deep-down escape from reality, heart-pumping passion, and love for the game. We go for the "W" every time!

But what happens when you have a physical setback during the offseason? A torn ACL, ankle, or shoulder? A major illness or disease? A neck or back injury? Can you recover before the season? If not, then what? I know this all too well—from coming off my season high with a personal setback to having a major season low with "breaking" my C1 in my spinal cord. If you do not know how important the C1 is to your spinal cord, head, and neck, think of it as the top of your spine that protects your cervical nerve roots to your brain, aka the "communication wires" to your brain, and helps with your movements (front, back, side to side).

Setback to the Comeback

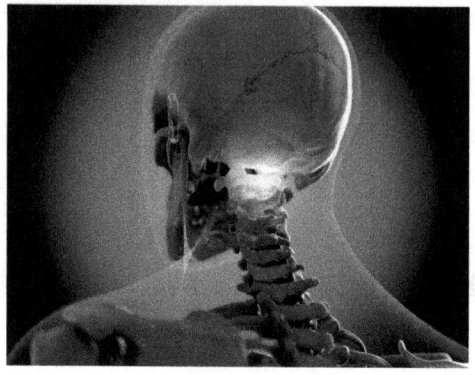

Without a fully functioning spine, you could lose your ability to walk or feel, or in extreme circumstances, die. By now, I am sure you understand the C1 is extremely important for basic human life, let alone competitive sports.

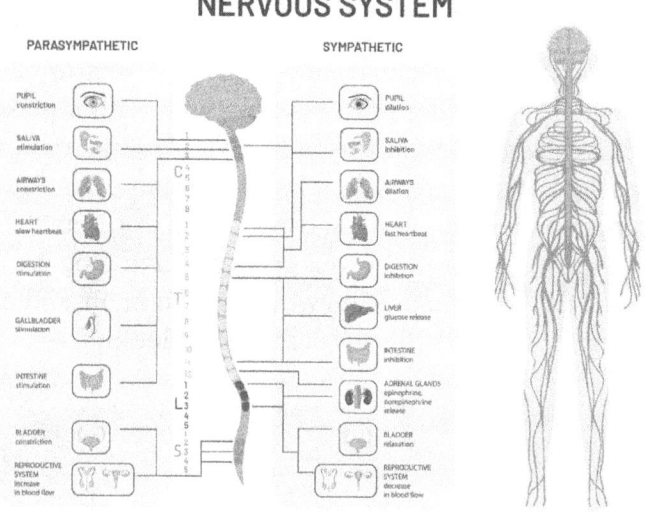

I will never forget fall ball in '08. We (Pitt softball) played a practice tournament in Ohio. We were in between games and wanted to stay loose so we decided to play a game called "pepper": a simple warmup game where you toss the ball, and the batter tries to hit it down, but if they pop it up and you catch it, you get to bat. A silly game, but it gets the blood flowing. Picture this: The team is in a U-shape around the batter, and the ball pops up close to me. I see it clearly, dive full out, realize I overestimated, try to correct mid-dive, fall on my neck, and SNAP like a chicken bone popping. [BLACK OUT.] I am going to tell you what I do remember. I did not just lose feeling right away; I had sharp pains catapulting up to my brain followed by the feeling you get when your body falls asleep (ants crawling) and then NOTHING, literally nothing. I went through what felt like an eternity but was closer to a 15- to 30-second full-body paralysis. Before I blacked out, I was told my scream was piercing. Me, screaming? I have one of the highest tolerances for pain, but what happened that day was a catastrophic injury. There was no flash before me, just merely waking up, a trainer stabilizing my neck, medics driving on the field.

Ready for this? In the middle of being put on a stretcher in the middle of the softball field, all I could think about was three major things. First, call my professor. I had an organic chemistry test the following day. Second, do not cut my No. 3 uniform; it needs to stay intact for the season. And lastly, do not call my mom!

Think about that. My priorities meant that there were no excuses when it came to excelling on and off the field, a key athletic building block that differentiates us. It was an obsession to prove to the academic community that athletes have a place in science (we are not just jocks) and to the athletic world you can be a "nerd" and major in what you want, not what fits your schedule (make it work). Here I am once again working to take on the world again, trying to prove everything to everyone else (working on it to this day). I also knew

I was getting back in the uniform, so I made the medics swear to me they would not cut me out of the uniform. I knew I had to put an "avatar" on to handle my fears and refocus on the recovery, whatever that may look like. There was no doubt when I got feeling again, laying on the open field, neck stabilized and vulnerable, that I was going to play again, period. And lastly, I did not want to worry my family because I was going to do what needed to be done in whatever manner it needed to be done. I have always had a winner's mentality; it is who I am and what makes me tick.

Straight to the local hospital I went. Everyone knew the plan that cutting my uniform was not an option, but they did call my mom from what looked like a satellite phone from the ambulance. My first words to my mom: "I am okay. They think I broke my head. All good, don't come." Can you imagine being on the other side of that phone? Geez, the things I put my mom and dad through while I was on my WINNING missions in life! No emotional intelligence that day, but all good. I learned that a little later on.

I must have met 20 different people in a series of two to four hours. Machine after machine, but no one was really talking to me, which scared me for a while. I was trying to figure out if I could decipher the "medical professional" jargon. All I wanted to know was something, anything. Instead, I was met with unknown, my mind taking over and thinking it was all bad news ahead. But my winner mentality was constantly checking my "avatar" back in line: "Not the time to be unbalanced." *The big key to injuries is don't put negative into the situation; deal with the reality.*

The Pitt medical staff on site was everything; I had blind trust in whatever they told me to do. They navigated the conversations, and I stayed level headed, but I wanted to scream and cry so bad. WHY ME? WHY NOW? I lost track of time when they put morphine in me. I had told them all I needed was IV fluids and no funny meds. I felt like I was having such an out-of-body experience, as it seemed like I was the key focus, but I was also a third person at the same time. A good way to think about it is when you go to classes and others in the class are talking about you loud enough for you to hear it like you are not in the room. It's an odd feeling that many athletes feel as well as celebrities. It comes with the territory sometimes.

I failed the IV and morphine fight but felt all was good when they told me I was fine, just swollen. The Pitt medical staff is the best of the best, and my trainer looked at me with stern seriousness and said, "Put the neck brace on, and you will not take it off until you go to our medical staff." They knew my neck injury was not one to mess with and wanted multiple specialists' opinions. It was a tone that I understood clearly. All I thought in my head was "Welcome to your new Day 1. Do what they say to a T."

No big deal. After the game, the team picked me up in the travel bus at the hospital. Just a normal Tuesday. The game changed! I now had to learn how to lead from the back until I got cleared. Step one was walking on the bus, joking, letting the team throw their jabs, so they could see I was okay and coming back soon. This is where human behavior, situational leadership, and body language matters most. I didn't have time to have my "off day." My new Day 1 started in the ambulance, so I worked through the mental road ahead immediately. Just because I got hurt didn't make me less of a captain. In fact, it became more important. Razor-focusing on the situation at hand and putting your personal feelings to the side takes every bit of grit and character. I sat in the front of the bus with this neck brace while my neck was cramping more and more as the morphine wore off.

As we got back Pitt, I immediately went to the doctors at UPMC. I bypassed everyone in the waiting room, and all

I could feel were cold stares from others who were thinking, *Oh, she is an athlete getting special treatment, but it sucks to be her with that neck brace on.* As I said earlier, it is always YOU versus YOU. Many won't understand, some will have an opinion, but all I was focused on was Day 2—nothing else mattered. The MRI couldn't give a good picture, as I was still extremely swollen, so I had to wear the neck brace for two more weeks.

I never envisioned being fitted for a "more comfortable" gel foam neck brace. Sitting in class was unbearable because of the stationary position, not being able to look down to take notes, and intense migraines that came at random times. I refused pain meds! I wanted to mentally stay sharp in class. I would come early and stay late in class to meet with my professors on how we could partner to ensure I did not miss any deliverables, actively participated, but had the courage to know when I needed to rest. The effort and care I showed through this adversity happened to be inspiring to my professors and classmates. So much so that many students and teachers allowed the recording of the class or sharing voice notes so I wouldn't miss the lesson.

My whole life changed. I had to be more auditory-focused because it was hard to look down to write. I was a better visual learner, so I had to learn to adjust how I retained information. To this day, I am beyond grateful for others showing empathy—truly remarkable. Empathy is okay, but please be careful not to allow "being babied," because that can lead to bad habits and tolerating problems. I was fortunate, as I was shown pure empathy served with a slice of "humble pie." Eating was difficult, and food would get stuck in the neck brace while I ate with the team. Some days I would just want to cry.

The question "Who am I outside of sports?" came to me daily. I felt useless. I couldn't focus, eat, or play ball. In these moments, I tried to find my avatar, aka my alter ego, to get through the day and not let my teammates know how mentally strained I was.

Two weeks passed; I finally was able to get an MRI! I already knew how weak my neck was going to be after taking that neck brace off. Think about it: Your neck provides stability and range of motion for your head. Not using it for an extended period of time would definitely result in major weakness to overcome. I was watching the team practice from the bench in December, showing my support, watching the flow of the team, thinking about my organic chemistry final ahead, and my trainer came out. She said, "Sam, we have bad news. You broke your C1. Come with me immediately." [PAUSE]

My world felt like it was collapsing on me. This was supposed to be my repeat year, my senior year! I wanted to go for "player of the year" and end my career on a high note. Maybe even try out for the national team. [PAUSE] There I was, thinking, back to Day 1, yet again. I was losing hope and positivity, but then I thought I could either let this define me or overcome it. I chose to overcome. This illustrated my winner's mentality. I tapped into the only thing I had left, my innate power to create a new championship routine by setting goals, not tolerating my problem, assessing where I should go and why, laying a new foundation, and executing. Game time!

I couldn't sleep or shower without this neck brace, so you can imagine the strategic placement of pillows and plastic bags I had to engineer. About eight weeks went by, and I was set to do another MRI and X-ray as the inflammation was fully down. You ready for this?

I was born without my C1 fully intact, a congenital anomaly (aka defect)! A congenital anomaly on the C1 means a partial defect from birth that was benign (not harmful). I had the absence of the posterior arch, which looked like I was missing a full piece of my C1. With all the swelling, the doctors only noticed the abnormality after my body recovered. In the illustration below by radiopardia.org, I recall being a D.

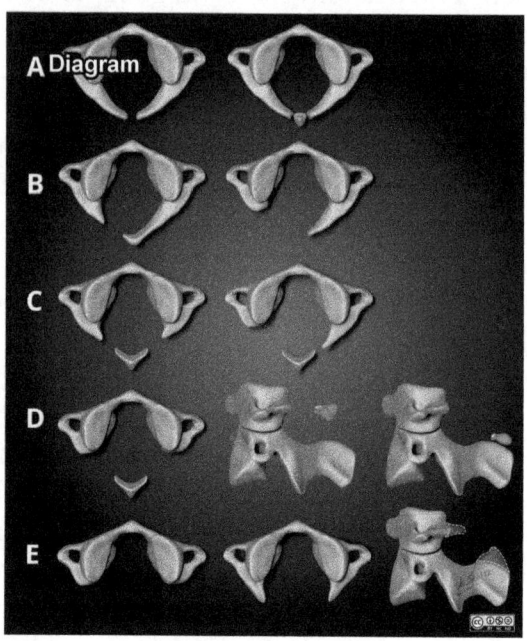

Source: Desai, P., Bell, D. Congenital anomalies of the posterior atlas arch. Reference article, Radiopaedia.org. (accessed on 17 Jan 2022) https://doi.org/10.53347/rID-7766

I wish I was making this story up, but it is every bit of the truth. The doctors, medical staff, and trainers were shocked! I am sure I could be a case study in one of the medical books. Who knows?!

Let's level set. I am two months behind, neck weak, and captain going from my breakout year into my senior season. What next? You know the deal, yet again: another "Day 1" and modifying my championship routine. I was ready for whatever was ahead. Conditioning three times a day and pronation, protraction, and retraction therapy (all things neck, spine, strength, and posture) were the wave (it was painful at first). Ice baths, warm compression, constantly challenging my physical thresholds, and throwing up during conditioning all to get to game day in February. On my first day back post-release from the doctors, we had a long team run (remember, I was a 3- and 4-hitter—I liked to jog around the bases) followed by a sprint up the steep hill. They called this hill "Cardiac Hill" for a reason. All through the run and sprint up, I was "past" my physical threshold, but as you know, our bodies can do a lot more than we think they can. We as athletes are built for it! It is all a mental game. So, I was throwing up the whole way, but NEVER STOPPED or QUIT!

I will never again ask, "Why me?" **The setbacks for the comebacks are the hardest mentally but the best learning opportunities. In order to achieve greatness in your sport, career, and life, you need to understand how setbacks and failing fast over and over are where the breakthroughs emerge.** Changing your mentality is not easy, but what you know how to do well is find a way. You do this every day through trying to get the starting spot on the field, getting through a hard midterm or final, and making it through weights, practice, school, and study hall. You find a way to make it work and get it done.

As an athlete, if you are weak on one part of your game, you practice, fail, do it over and over until you get it right. The goal should always be to get 1% better every day. Work with others who do it better (your approach will change—the bar is higher), stay coachable, and do not be afraid to fail. You may be classified as the best in your sport or space, but I promise you, there is someone out there who is waiting for you to have your "off day." I, along with other savage, elite high-performers, are looking for your off day, every day, so be careful what your off day looks like! It isn't a threat; it is a way of life. Records are made to be broken, bars are meant to be raised, elevation requires separation, and closing the gap is necessary when you aspire to success in all aspects of your life.

> **Records are made to be broken, bars are meant to be raised, elevation requires separation, and closing the gap is necessary when you aspire to success in all aspects of your life.**

You apply this in your sports career, so why not leverage this tool and muscle memory as you navigate your success post-sports? It is who you are! When you change your frame of reference, learn from the best, and bridge the gap with other levelers, the rooms you enter, conversations you have, intentions you take, actions you lead, and results you generate change!

What are you going to tell yourself: When it gets hard, you quit? Nope, not ever! We do not roll like that. The way we live our lives as athletes is second to none. Many want to replicate it, but it's extremely difficult to duplicate. This is yet another athlete advantage in your toolbox. I can't wait to show you how we are going to put your athlete advantage in overdrive and catapult your legacy during and post-sports! I am fired up! This right here excites me! I am passionate about all things YOU + SUCCEEDING! LET'S GO!

Disclaimer: If you are a quitter, please put this book down. This is not for you.

Success Beyond Game Day Playbook Recap:

Physical Setback to the Comeback: Overcoming the Controllable and Uncontrollable

1. **Go beyond setting goals** on Day 1. Sign them, and now you have a contract.
   a. When you have your physical setback, feeling like you are at Day 1 again, add some short- to medium-term attainable goals to keep you focused and see some early wins.
   b. Let some of your goals be tangible and measurable. For me, I just wanted to move my neck left and right. I wasn't trying to move a mountain, but it was a short-term goal that was critical to my next steps.
   c. Try to get more comfortable with asking for help, even when you are pushing through. The best success comes when you enlist the right help at the right time.

2. **Identify the problem. Do not tolerate problems**, aka red flags.
   a. Physical setbacks become more mental than physical. Recognize that early on you need a game plan. Do not just fight through it by yourself. Include your trainers, coaches, teammates, teachers, and relationships.
   b. Be careful when making decisions or reacting too fast. Pause. Resist your urge to respond immediately.
   c. A level head is always best, so take a breather. Never make an important life decision when you are extremely happy, sad, or upset. Trust me on this one!

d. Sometimes you need to flex and lead from the back; take on a new role for the betterment of the team. Enable others to step up and show out! ELEVATE!
3. **Peel back the layers** and go below the surface. Ask yourself the six whys.
   a. It is a bad couple of days or months, not a bad life. Recognize the difference.
   b. If you build the right game plan, you will shift your focus to getting back 150% versus worrying about rushing rehab because someone is going to take your spot.
   c. Grow through what you go through and feel all the feels. Learn how you respond to your triggers. Adapt! Embrace your moments of solitude.
4. **Lay the groundwork and foundation** with optionality and flexibility.
   a. Every day you must get 1% better. The comeback is a beautiful thing. I never said it was an easy thing. But within the setback, you learn about yourself in a way that most never do. Leverage that!
   b. When you build your game plan and you have further setbacks, pause and be open-minded. Stay hyper-focused and disciplined. Allow the experts to help you drive new options and pathways for recovery. Be flexible and nimble!
5. **Flawless operationalization**. Game time!

4

Your Athlete Advantage

Catapulting Zero Years of "Work Experience" (Black Hole Feeling)

The road to Easy Street goes through the sewer.

—John Madden

You learn a lot about who you are as a person when you are faced with adversity and must overcome what you believe, at the time, is the "impossible." Where yesterday's success is today's new starting point with a sprinkle of "Can you do it faster?" You learn about your inner grit, character, and perseverance. You begin to shift to another gear, one that you didn't know existed, and learn how to broaden your leverage from your setback to comeback. Then, you graduate.

Now what? Do you know life without sports? I didn't. What can you do when you graduate (crickets chirping in the background)? What happens if you graduate when the economy is struggling? The real world hits you like a brick wall, fast and hard! What next? Do you feel prepared? I wasn't. Have you ever worked a day outside of sports in your life? I didn't. Who are you outside of sports? Will you matter to anyone? Do you lose your "stock value"? How will you cope without someone telling you where and when to be there?

Welcome back to your new Day 1! The empty space and dark void-like feeling is the scariest part of graduating as an athlete—or anyone, for that matter. You feel the inescapable gravitational weight of the unknown, your new reality, anxiety, and lack of purpose. Your strength will be challenged, but there is so much light at the end of the tunnel! Be open and receptive to your feelings, but do not let your feelings drive your actions! Avoid making decisions when you are sad, mad, or extremely happy. When you are in the thick of "all the feels," embrace them, breathe, walk away, and come back to your decision table.

You have spent your entire life learning and building yourself into an elite athlete. You are an expert in all things "whatever it takes" to make it to the 'ship! This is applicable to all parts of your life, so step up and broaden your experiential learning leverage. YOU KNOW WHAT IT TAKES TO BE A WINNER! Say it often, especially when you have moments when you realize that you are no longer on the roster. You will have identity issues, and in these times, you must remember you are built for championship wins and overcoming losses. Your new wins and overcoming losses will just be in a different package. This is not your first rodeo.

Of course, you will have days when you question who you are and if you matter post-sports. You are human! You grew up putting on a show for others' entertainment, and now what?! It sounds dark, but it is the genuine truth of being an elite, hyper-focused athlete. We grow up practicing and obsessing over making it to the top, but once you graduate or even retire from the top, who are you outside of sports? I ask the question again because I am confident that if I were standing in front of you right now, you would not be able to consistently articulate who you are and what your brand embodies. How do I know that? I have been there, felt all the feels, fumbled in my identity post-sports, and made it to the other side as a trailblazer in business. Branding and marketing are two of the most important tools you will need to master during and after your sports career. Lucky for you, I am here to help!

Thinking about life post-sports can happen all at once or hit you randomly throughout your career. For me, it hit me all at once! In these moments, you get to truly see who you are outside of sports. You get to decide if you become a hero or a zero. Yet again, "you versus you." Remember, proper planning prevents piss poor performance. Setting intentional goals (visible every day) and digging deep to understand "all things you" and "why" enables you to begin testing new waters. From there you learn how you build off of your current foundation (trial and error) and execute!

When I say "testing new waters," I am suggesting you jump in, just like you would an ice bath post-game for recovery. If you go in slowly, you drag out the cold chill, raised goosebumps, and back-of-the-neck-hair-standing-up pain instead of allowing your body to adapt quicker to the shock, not to mention the mental piece. Jump in, recover, and repeat each workout or postgame life and learning. It helps you overcome from being "sore" and mitigates your brain taking over. It convinces you to "take a day off" that you didn't really need. If you don't jump in at all, the lactic acid takes over like a slow-drip IV with morphine; you can barely walk or extend your T-rex-like arms because you are that sore. I don't know about you, but I would get most sore two days after an intense workout or game. I learned quickly that an ice bath was an asset, even if post-recovery included me having to walk in the snow home. Working smarter, not harder doesn't always feel glamorous, but it pays dividends! The best way to think about "paying back dividends" means you can see advantages in a later time period. That time period can be short-, medium-, or long-term paybacks. In the example above, you get in an ice bath, as it will pay dividends for your body, prevent you from being sore, and enable you to notch it up in the next practice or game. On the financial side, dividends are one of the many ways you can make money while you sleep. You'll see benefits and advantages that come later on by choices you make today.

Intention and consistency set you up for a stronger start the next day. When you realize the power of the ice bath and your improved performance output, you begin to shift your mindset to see it as a tool for success, less of a punishment.

Once you know the results, you translate that to value, and you go a little harder the next day. Do you see what I am getting at here? All about value creation in every aspect of your life.

You will fall, feel like a failure, learn, and repeat often during and post-sports. The key here is failing fast (not tolerating problems), arming yourself with new learnings, and translating the new information into intrinsic value. Think about "intrinsic value" as an asset (YOU) that holds value no matter the external circumstances. Later in the book we will take a deep dive into all things you, asset generation, and wealth preservation! We will explore how you can acquire assets and create value and how risk, with controls, can translate into financial wealth with long-term lucrative opportunities. You get to decide if you want to fall into the normal pack or leverage your beast mode and create new runways. It is up to you! Lucky for you, I chose beast mode + new runways! Buckle up!

My personal journey is one for the books. Imagine graduating with a chemistry degree, having put in countless hours in study hall and office hours to keep an edge, then having no idea what you want to do with it. Welcome to my Day 1 post-sports. It was 2009, in the middle of the global financial crisis, the most destructive occurrence since the Great Depression, headed toward the Great Recession. The global financial crisis was a stressful time around the world, especially for the financial industry, where most of the banks around the world were headed for bankruptcy as they were overleveraged and needed government intervention. Banks offered cheap credit and loose loan borrowing, which in turn made the real estate bubble pop, and then came the recession. I am not here to give you a history lesson, but rather to show you that I graduated in a rough period. I would recommend you fully understand the global financial crisis and Great Recession because history does have a way of repeating itself.

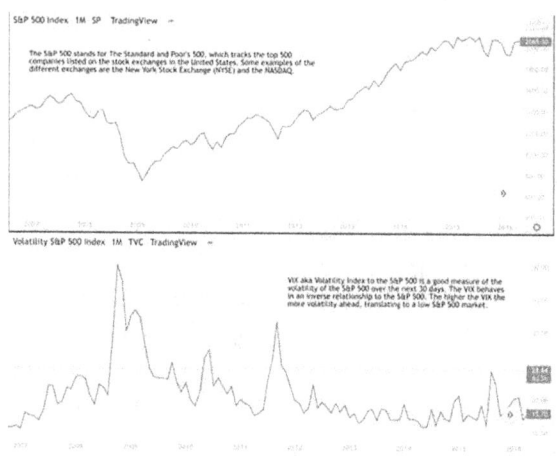

I was terrified. I experienced a complete loss of identity and felt clueless about the road ahead. I didn't sleep for two weeks straight. The thought of "What is next?" consumed me!

At the end of my Pitt softball career, the economy was an absolute mess, softball was out of the Olympics after the 2008 Games in Beijing, and professional softball was not a full-time option. I was clueless about what I was going to do with a chemistry degree and zero years of "traditional" work experience. Imagine being asked to recreate your resume as a graduating senior, and all you can do is stare at a blank sheet of paper for three hours. I felt lost, with the walls closing in on me, just like in the hospital with my neck injury a year prior. As you can imagine, it took a lot of inner soul-searching and taking a step back to assess my broader experiential learning leverage. Remember, I had been there, done that, so I chose to reframe my mindset and turn it into a challenge. You know the deal: My muscle memory and winner mentality took over. How you do anything is how you do everything. I chose greatness no matter the journey.

I have always prided myself on being prepared and embracing ambiguity, but this transition was tough. I did not know who I was post-sports. So, I took myself back to the 305, my hometown, Miami, Florida, for the summer and treated it like a training program back to the top. I called it the "humble pie" season. I barely talked to anyone. I was hyper-focused on "Who am I post-sports?" and "What are my long-term goals?" What I realized quickly was that I did not have a true long-term plan.

My "long-term" goals were:

1. Get a full scholarship.

2. Win championships.

3. Play at the highest level possible.

I somehow convinced myself that majoring in chemistry was a good idea because it was difficult, not because of what the degree would afford me. Sound familiar to your moves? Or did you major in something that fit your athletic schedule? Or are you majoring in something that your parents wanted you to do?

All I know is that I felt like I had failed because I went back home without a next step and a fancy Bachelor of Science degree. Each day, I started to shift into action, knowing it too would pass. I am a winner. I know how to overcome and elevate. I was working out two to three times a day, eating clean, and working toward my new championship routine. I was harnessing the familiar, my comfort—an athletic routine surrounded by all things planned—each day to get a sense of purpose and system back. After 28 days, my mindset and approach started getting back to that of an elite athlete. And just like that, one day it hit me! I knew I could leverage my chemistry degree in multiple ways, all with a common thread, business.

Some of the ideas that came to mind were to work for a pharmaceutical company, hospital management, sports management, or industrial business management, and/or as a doctor, softball coach, or nutritionist. I cast the net wide and felt unlimited possibilities. *I was growing through what I was going through, and just like that, the plan crystallized.* I knew I needed to get a better grip on business fundamentals. Why not go back to school? The economy was not great, and I still had that edge to take on classes. I was going to find my way, rain or shine. Eureka to my new Day 1 post-sports!

Within one month, I maintained my workout routine and started to take classes at the University of Miami to prep for the GMAT, a requirement for MBA programs. Every night I would study! You know, study on how to take the test, less on knowing the actual concepts. Many of the concepts I knew, but I always managed to negotiate why the wrong answer was right! This time, I changed it up and took another approach: Learn how to beat the test. A good example is the NFL Combine for NFL Draft prospects. There is a smorgasbord of drills that football players spend postseason learning for that one day (or weekend), with the notion that they do it 150% because it is their "Pro Day interview." I understand why they pay trainers thousands of dollars to get them Combine ready, but maybe just a few of the physical tests are applicable?

Success Beyond Game Day

To all the NFL players and coaches, when I see you around, let's debate it! Think about it: Does an offensive lineman need to run the 40-yard dash in Spanx in a certain time? When (not if) there is a turnover in the NFL, and magically that O-lineman has their 10 seconds of "fame in the fast lane," they either drop because most players that recover fumbles are taught that (plus, not many can strip the ball from the "big boys"), or they get gassed after 20 yards, where the defense catches up and tackles them. But, hey, they train for what the Combine requires. So, I had the same approach. I studied on how to best beat the test and get noticed. I had the skills and will; all I needed was the chance.

In parallel, I contacted my alma mater, specifically the Pitt Life Skills Program, and tapped into the athletic alumni connections. It took me too long to address my problem and ask for help. That was such a great learning. It was a major area in my life that I had to intentionally work on, as it did not come naturally. It is all about working smarter, not harder! A good way to think about this is when you are in a team sport and you must flex the way you communicate and ask for support and/or influence, depending on the person or situation. Sometimes you just need to ask a teammate who is better or sees the game differently than you in an area for help. Asking for help shows respect for their craft and gets you closer to closing the gap in the skill you need. Sometimes we think help is a sign of weakness, when in reality it is a true sign of strength. Mentorship, collaboration, and coaching are some of the best ways you can sharpen your iron. Only iron can sharpen iron. And the only thing that negatively impacts iron is itself.

> **Mentorship, collaboration, and coaching are some of the best ways you can sharpen your iron. Only iron can sharpen iron. And the only thing that negatively impacts iron is itself.**

Being independent and a go-getter doesn't mean you can't accept help! This has been an area where I had to spend a lot of energy and time "peeling back the layers" to get to my "below the surface" and challenge why I tolerated problems (aka red flags). As athletes, we strive to be the ones called upon but challenge yourself to not let your pride dictate how you move. I ask you to learn from my shortcomings and let your coachability drive your ship. These are some of the strongest tools you have in your toolbox. To get to the collegiate and pro level you need to be coachable. Without that, you have no shot at lasting in the program. I am also confident that you have been humbled once or twice in your sports career. We were all rookies at one time or another!

Fast forward through a month of getting myself in line. I took my GMAT at the tail end of summer. By leveraging my athletic network at Pitt, I had connected with a key director of the Pitt MBA program who knew firsthand the value and successful mentality of athletes. He gave me targets to hit and asked me to let him know when I was applying. My target was to start January 2010 because I had missed the August 2009 window. He was honest with me all the way through and said that it would not be easy. He pre-wired me that my acceptance would take a lot of convincing to the board because I did not have any "traditional" work experience. One of the values of an MBA program is that it offers interactive cross-pollination among peers in different roles and companies to help you further hone new skills needed to climb your success ladder. Here I was, with zero years of work experience, trying to get in with a conservative executive crowd and one champion influencer. There wasn't one day as I was interviewing for my chance that I doubted my value in that program. I went 150% all-in. All it takes is one YES! You can have 1,000 nos, but all you need is one yes! I started to truly understand how someone championing on your behalf was the golden nugget to shortening the window toward success.

For me, it was about the business playoffs. I never wanted anything more than a sports championship, until I made it to the business playoffs. Every day I was working out and waiting for the acceptance letter or the phone call saying, "You are in." I got a phone call, but it wasn't "You got in!" Instead, I was asked to be interviewed in front of the conservative, all-male executive panel. So conservative that you often hear a "no" before "yes" or even "challenges" before "opportunities." To the average person, this may have been bad news, but to me, I lived for it! These are the rare moments where you put up or shut up. I am not about the settle up; I am all about the level up! If you know, you know.

I was put through multiple phone and in-person interviews. The clever part was there were some interviews scheduled and some not. Sometimes they would show up late and have me wait. They tested me, but I didn't care because I was in the room! I had a voice! I knew every day was an interview, so I lived for the moments I got to connect and drive my brand. Picture a high-profile legal courtroom with everyone staring, the media already convicting you of a crime you didn't commit, and expect yourself to stay poised. This was me, the athlete, who wanted her chance post-game day.

I was excited and nervous, just like on game day. I knew how to control my emotions, lead with intentional poise, and go for the win! All these interviews were not standard protocol, but with each interview, I knew that I was one step closer. A key to remember: You must be careful at the end of every conversation. Just like a legal proceeding, it is that moment where the defense attorney turns away to walk back to their bench and causally turns back to you last minute and says, "Just one more question." Do not ever get comfortable! Be prepared. A lot of twists and turns happen, which means your endurance comes into major play during interviews. Treat it like a game. You play 150% in every second of play, even if you are in triple OT. If not, the other team is waiting for your "off" moment. You, as an athlete, don't have the luxury to have an off moment because you were tired! Same concept here; these interviews were headed toward OT.

Always know you will have skeptics. What I did was focus on my champions and supporters in the room, while showing respect and entertaining the skeptics (never ignore anyone). For the skeptics, I researched their backgrounds so I could find a good intersection and get them to talk about themselves. Remember, work smarter, not harder! Understanding human behavior is a major asset in your toolbox. People like to talk about themselves—fact! Not every executive panel member thought it was a good idea, but they still were willing to give me five minutes. BOOM! *Always know when you have leverage and use it fully!*

Do not sleep on what I just said there: You have five minutes, and you must utilize your leverage to get and stay in the room. Many times, with influential and/or executive leaders, you have about one minute (really 30 seconds) to grab their attention. You have about two minutes to translate who you are and why it matters. And in your final two minutes, you have to make a call to action and get them in your corner.

A total of five minutes to translate your "stock worth"! The way I define stock worth is the total value of you the brand. It is bigger than sports. It is your qualitative and quantitative measure of all things you, today, tomorrow, and in the future, at any point in time, valued based off the present view of it all. This pumps me up!

Part of why I get excited is that I have always been a people pleaser. I turned my bias and weakness into a strength. Learning how to please different people with different opinions and motivations was an area where I excelled. I live for being in the thick of ambiguity! As one of my mentors has eloquently taught me, you need to be relatable, relevant, and reliant and have rapport.

Every interaction was my chance. I didn't focus on the fact that they needed to talk to me multiple times to decide on the viability of my admission into the program. I never once thought about the "no." I stayed consistent in my message and hyper-focused on how I could leverage my athletic background into the business world. Every conversation ended with me saying, "I will be your best bet. I will be at the highest levels of a Fortune 100 company one day." Every single time we spoke, I reiterated that. I explained how being an athlete is a business and I am more than equipped to add value to the program. I am the differentiator. I am the future success story.

After three panel discussions and multiple individual calls, I received an email. The rest became history. Not only did I make it in, but I accomplished everything I said. To this day, many of those panel members reach out from time to time to check in on me. Skeptics turned into fans. Oh, not to mention, my first job was working for a Fortune 100 company ($40B dollar company, to be exact)! After this one YES, I turned myself into a global "best bet" business leader on the fast senior executive track!

Now the real fun begins. You get to leverage my learnings to see how you can get "in the room" full of skeptics or supporters and use your athlete advantage to drive success. I found a path, so I challenge you to break my record and raise the bar! This is what the champion routine is all about!

Let's go!

Success Beyond Game Day Playbook Recap:

Your Athlete Advantage: *Catapulting Zero Years of "Work Experience" (Black Hole Feeling)*

1. **Go beyond setting goals** on Day 1. Sign them, and now you have a contract.
   a. Set a routine in place to give you a sense of "known." No one is telling you where to be and when to be there any longer, so you can get overwhelmed on how best to manage your day. Trust me! (Little win area.)
   b. Shift goals to purpose-driven, intentional, and short-term quick wins to go after.
   c. Start to write down who you are beyond sports. You will struggle through this, but get it on paper. Transitioning to establishing your brand positioning is key. (Prepare!!!)

2. **Identify the problem. Do not tolerate problems,** aka red flags.
   a. Find areas where you can leverage your athletic skills acquired (physical and mental) versus areas of struggle. I bet you have a lot more to leverage than not, when no detail is left unturned. This will set you up for the real personal and professional brand build-out and the next steps!

    b. Check your emotions; it is humble pie season! Be poised even when you just want to scream. This is when you start to feel the pain of running a marathon. Overcome!
    c. Every day is an interview and your chance to get where you need to be. Focus on getting your headspace ready even though you don't feel great about it. Push through.
    d. Being vulnerable and lost is okay; "feel all the feels." It's all about consistency, getting 1% better every day, and fostering a routine of familiarity to get some "comfort" back.
    e. You do not need to do this on your own. Find a strong ambassador willing to help you, especially in your weaker skill areas. Champions on your behalf will become one of your best leverage points. (Arm yourself.)

3. **Peel back the layers** and go below the surface. Ask yourself the six whys.
    a. In the middle of your "identity crisis," ask why you feel the way you do. Go deep, deep.
    b. You only have a finite amount of time to translate your "stock worth" to future champions on your behalf (or executives). Just know, it starts with grabbing their attention, followed by laying out who you are and why you matter to them, and finally giving your call to action to get them in your corner.
    c. If you do not like where you are, change and pivot. No one is going to hand this to you. It's every bit of you versus you this season!

4. **Lay the groundwork and foundation** with optionality and flexibility.
   a. Remember, it takes one yes, one door, or one opportunity to change your growth trajectory.
   b. You bring a lot to the table; do not negotiate with yourself. Opportunities before challenges!
   c. Mentorship, collaboration, and coaching are some of the best ways you can sharpen your iron. Only iron can sharpen iron. And the only thing that negatively impacts iron is itself.

5. **Flawless operationalization.** Game time!
   a. Did you notice how I never talked about having "zero" years of work experience? It is a moot point when you refocus and start to see how much more you have (and are capable of).
   b. You are a seasonable professional in the athletic world; you have tons of experience! LEVERAGE!

5

Your Post-Sports Afterglow

Be the Neck, Not the Head

I've missed more than 9,000 shots in my career. I've lost almost 300 games. Twenty-six times I've been trusted to take the game-winning shot and missed. I've failed over and over and over again in my life. And that is why I succeed.

—Michael Jordan

Who are you beyond sports? Get used to that question. I want to make sure that, as you build your legacy roadmap, you are continuously improving that answer. If you have it figured out, could you translate "all things you" in two minutes or less? Remember, best case, you only have five minutes to illustrate your brand and captivate your audience (aka the elevator pitch). Once you hit a goal, do you spend the time to create new ones? Or do you get comfortable when the game starts to slow down as you move from rookie to senior? Are you so hyper-focused on success that you tend to be narrow-minded with no view of your peripherals? I am about to walk you through some essential tools that will help you break yourself down and build yourself back up. It all starts with a true open mentality and shifting from "yes, but" to "yes, and." More on this later in the book. We are about to dive into being the neck, not the head. You know, your post-sports afterglow.

You may be thinking, what does that even mean, and why should you entertain it? Well, it is literal and simple. Can you move your head without your neck? No! In Chapter 3 I illustrated my literal struggle with my C1 spinal cord injury. Your C1 provides stability for your neck so you can rotate up and down or side to side. Your neck holds your head in place and affords the flexibility to see all around, which your head alone could not do. Now think of the times when you've had headaches. Often, you have been able to push through, but if you slept wrong on your neck or snapped your neck like a chicken bone popping like I did, your whole day changes. Your neck is quintessential to you and your ability to function in your daily life.

On the other hand, it is also a single point of failure. If something happens to your neck, you only have one (uncontrollable) reality! Being the neck, not the head, is what you as an athlete should embody. You should provide stability for yourself and others (emphasis on YOURSELF), be flexible and nimble in your mission, and handle the ups and downs.

> **If something happens to your neck, you only have one (uncontrollable) reality! Being the neck, not the head, is what you as an athlete should embody. You should provide stability for yourself and others (emphasis on YOURSELF), be flexible and nimble in your mission, and handle the ups and downs.**

We will work through strengthening your "neck" and work through your single points of failure. Building you up can then turn into you helping build up others, but keep a pulse on whether you're "helping" versus "being a crutch" for others. We are going to get you equipped to build your current and future team up so your bench strength is bionic!

Success Beyond Game Day

I am driving you toward focusing on the important aspects of personal and professional growth while never losing track of your journey's peripherals. The way to think about peripherals is staying focused on a goal but being open to seeing opportunities that come at different times without impacting your forward focus. You should see the difference between single points of failure and more degrees of freedom. I want you to be prepared to know when you should tap in versus when you should pass, getting you to a place where you are comfortable with establishing a pipeline of opportunities and staying disciplined to them. I want you to know how to dominate when you are at the top and dominate as you climb the ladder. I want to help you understand your failure modes and how to dig deep, go below the surface, and course correct if needed. These are critically important concepts. Let's dive in!

We all have a story and different paths we take as athletes. The same applies post-sports. One of the aspects of success is it can become obsessive. When is it ever enough? Once you win a state title, then you want to win a national title and then a global title. Once you make your first $100K, then you want $1M, followed by $5M and then $10M, followed by $100M and maybe even $1B. In business, you may get promoted to manager, but then you want to be a director, followed by VP and SVP and C-suite.

Success is an obsessive moving target, and sometimes it gets lonely. Just as lonely as you can get when fans talk good or bad about you in the same room, as they stare at you and then ask to take a picture. It may feel at times that others may treat you as a figment of their imagination and not as a real person. The water gets murky sometimes, but the glory is great! Let's be honest, some days you just want to be by yourself (no interviews or places to be), and maybe even have a mundane "off day." With being that "figment of their imagination" comes an unspoken expectation and new responsibility to be "superhuman." When you lose (we all lose/fail at least once), you can literally crush a person's hope or even the city's dream (depending on where you go to school). Think about that power!

> With being that "figment of their imagination" comes an unspoken expectation and new responsibility to be "superhuman." When you lose (we all lose/fail at least once), you can literally crush a person's hope or even the city's dream (depending on where you go to school). Think about that power!

It is more than sports. You impact lives. You are a living role model, a kid's hope and dream to find a way.

Your goals that you are living by today could be someone's dream; never sleep on that fact. There are only so many places up top, competition is cutthroat, and the air is thin! The chess

Success Beyond Game Day

game never ends—all strategy, all day. The more success you have, the more people rely on you while simultaneously trying to take your spot.

That is why understanding human behavior and what makes people tick is so important. When leading a corporation or business, you have people who spend more time with you than their families, just so their immediate families can have a "good life." In corporate America, the system is designed to keep the pedal down and keep you "drinking from the fire hydrant" busy so you don't have a chance to think about your peripherals, let alone ask for a raise. **In essence, you are accountable to not only provide a positive environment but also be a decision source for the livelihood of many people. You need to become the "people's champion."** Yet another example of why you as an athlete are built for this! You learned how to win and take losses at a young age. You have a lot of experiential learning and years of success thus far; leverage it! It is all about knowing who you are and branding that.

As you embark on what success beyond game day looks like for you, be intentional and lay out the next 20 years. Start with Year 1 and build five-year goals from there until you hit Year 20. You may be thinking, "I do not know who I am fully yet," or "How can I possibly think 20 years down the road?" I challenge that thought process. Perhaps the reason why you "do not know who you are yet" is because you have never sat down, truly and thoughtfully debated the pros and cons about what you want and why, and then wrote it down. Why? Because you thought you had time to do it. You may even be a bit scared to write it down because then it becomes more official. Exactly why I am asking you to do it now (no time like the present). Write it down, and work at it every day. **You will always be where you started if you do not take your first step, period.**

I am asking you to take your first step. Make your contract with yourself visible every day. If you don't write it down, nine times out of 10 it is out of sight, out of mind. Athletes live in the fast lane, coming up to breathe only when we absolutely need to, so let's break the cycle and change it up! We fear being replaced for taking an "off day," but setting time to establish your goals is not an "off day," but rather a critical step to generate the vision, navigate the pace, and hold yourself accountable for the results ahead. Shoot, this is your differentiator!

My Year 1 goal was to get international experience and make it into corporate America by 2012. All I knew was I was going to make it happen, no excuses. I made a contract with myself, so now I had to honor that. I had to pick the pace up. From 2010 to 2011, I went to job fairs all over the country, put on my hunter sales mentality, and utilized every resource from my undergrad to my MBA program. You don't have to start fresh; learn from others and reshape your approach. Once you experience your journey, give that wisdom to someone else. That is what a real leader does. Remember, it was the tail end of humble pie season; the tides were changing! Oh, the tides were changing!

If my goal was to gain international experience and make it to corporate America, what did I have to do? As you can imagine, it was as easy as 1, 2, and 3! Decision made overnight to live outside of the country ASAP! Lesson No. 1: I made an impulsive decision to live outside of the USA (big no-no). I didn't think about the potential language barriers, required visas needed, housing, currency exchange, or transportation ahead of me. But, hey, I saw a study abroad opportunity within my MBA grad program, and just like you would (right?), I jetted off within two months to Marseille, France, to go to EUROMED MARSEILLE Ecole de Management. Still insane when I think about it!

Success Beyond Game Day

So, I had never been to Europe, but traveled alone and did not know French to even ask for help if I needed it in an emergency. I had no idea where the embassy was or where I was directionally living; no lie, I was straight "winging" it. **Listen, I had a goal and tapped into my inner beast mode (aka my game day avatar) who doesn't understand halfway on anything. I did not embody proper planning, but with chaos comes reward (sometimes), right?** Lesson No. 2 is **do not negotiate or rationalize with yourself; just be prepared or recognize you missed the mark and improvise.** Sometimes you can learn by fire, but expect it will come with many unnecessary bumps in the road! This is definitely an area where you can control the outcomes better.

I wanted international experience, so I got on the plane, period. As a little side detail, I packed one suitcase of just shoes and the other with clothes. Seems backwards to me now but, hey, I was not thinking about the preparation, just mere willpower to make my contract come to fruition. Crazy thing is, I am not even that obsessed with shoes! I want you to picture six months with a ton of shoes, minimal clothes, a fresh passport, no French, and a look that screamed "She is American." This was me in Marseille. To anyone else it would be disaster, but to me, a new runway! All mindset!

Landed and off to a great start to Marseille, France—NOT! I got there early before the housing quarters were prepared for anyone, but there I was, with nowhere else to stay. I somehow found a person who knew enough broken English to let me in. I got into my apartment, and I didn't know I had needed to set up my electricity and Wi-Fi before I came. I swear that although I was an MBA student with a brain, I somehow lost all my sense leading up to this moment. I did not have power, Wi-Fi, water, food, or a means to get around. My ignorance was embarrassing. I didn't know if I could drink the water or not—basic information. I was naïve, ignorant, but ambitious. I went into survival mode. Lesson No. 3 is you grow through what you go through, but this could have been prevented. In the thick of it, you focus up. I somehow bartered my way to the store with a stranger. Should lesson No. 4 be stranger danger?

After things settled down, I started to get myself together. Met some great people, traveled, and started to see life outside of the US bubble. As an athlete, you know how to claw back when you're behind in the game, with a quarter, half, or inning to go. I made it work because I have been there, done that; it was just in a different package. I still chalk this up as a success with a dash of organized chaos. I got the checkmark on "international exposure," met some great people from all over the world, and learned a lot about myself! Upon my arrival back stateside, I took my former goals out, assessed if they still aligned with the vision, added more granularity, pivoted toward more long-term vision goals, and set up timelines. Goals are dreams with deadlines. If you do not put a date to it, you have a dream. If you put a deadline, step up; it's game time!

Back stateside, I worked as a graduate assistant for our Panther Club at Pitt. I was around the best of the best, from Hall of Famers to former athletes gone business elite; what could be better? I felt that I was in the right room every day. From the Panther Club to my MBA classes, I was respected and mentored by the best in the game! To this day, my dear friends—Sam Clancy Sr., Penny Semaia, Amy Niceswanger Anderson, and Charles Small—were a big part of my growth post-sports. They treated me as an equal and fostered an open environment for others to grow. I would do anything at any time for this group. They are a primary reason I decided to dive in headfirst in helping you succeed beyond game day.

Little did they know, I learned so much from merely watching and listening to how they "shaked and baked" across the athletic administration. I was like that one- or two-year-old who would play "shadow" with the adults and then ask "why?" Fifty times in a row. They always gave me a chance, fueled my curiosity, and opened the door. This team was (and still is) flawless! I have so much respect and honor having had the chance to be a part of their day-to-day! I am where I am today because of the doors they helped open!

> To this day, my dear friends—Sam Clancy Sr., Penny Semaia, Amy Niceswanger Anderson, and Charles Small—were a big part of my growth post-sports. They treated me as an equal and fostered an open environment for others to grow. I would do anything at any time for this group. They are a primary reason I decided to dive in headfirst in helping you succeed beyond game day.

This period in my life became more than just succeeding for myself. It morphed into ensuring excellence every

day so that everyone who spent the time to mentor, coach, and support me was proud! The key was to become their best return on investment (ROI) yet!

I had studied abroad, established the right mentors, leveraged the network, and aggressively attended career fairs. I was on the grind and had the right headspace for success. I lived and breathed the "all it takes is one yes!" mentality. At each career fair, I become quite proficient in translating my brand in five minutes or less, capturing many recruiters' attention. Every single conversation ended with, "You are a near-perfect candidate for our development program, articulate for your age, a former athlete from a big school, but it's just tough you have never had any real work experience." Oh, I have been down this road before, but the difference here was the recruiters' inability to look beyond their legacy criteria that was not with the current time.

I had a chemistry degree with a forthcoming MBA. I wanted to leverage both degrees, but the industrial sector is uber OLD SCHOOL (they want traditional experience). All confined to metrics, wanting to grow but too risk-averse to start, and hyper-focused on measuring the bell curve of people-talent-effectiveness. In my humble opinion, this is the ugly part of corporate America. It is important for you to understand your value and find unique ways to translate that. It was a blessing to be rejected by all the oil and gas, food, and pharma companies. It left me as a free agent with a big runway. I was never worried about being selected to work for a Fortune 100 company.

I was more aggravated that I traveled all over the country with no real translatable results to show for the effort. The learning here is about honing and tapping into your self-confidence, perseverance, and dedication, the key pillars of a successful athlete. Learning how to perfect my elevator pitch, exploring how I could tailor my messaging depending on the person, and finding better calls to action were my focus. One of the easiest things you can do is learn about who you are talking to and/or send a follow-up. Not just one follow-up, but randomly check in and show consistency. Of course, you should know about the company, but connecting with people in an authentic way is the key. Everyone has a different why, but we all have many areas of life's intersections that can lead to some of the strongest bridges and networks. Remember your network is your net worth! Always think about your stock value because you will be judged by the people you associate with, whether you like it or not! The best of the best leaders excel at understanding people (to the core), championing for people, and making necessary changes for people, period!

> **The best of the best leaders excel at understanding people (to the core), championing for people, and making necessary changes for people, period!**

Roll forward to a random day in March, and I received a LinkedIn message from a recruiter asking if I was interested in a new role that had never existed before in a Fortune 100 company. This is equivalent to how college coaches recruit on social media these days, quick and broad-reaching. There is little to no need to go out to a tournament unless it is for a specific purpose. I was suspect at first, but I had nothing to lose. I immediately responded that I was interested in taking a phone call, but I was walking in blind. Interestingly enough, she connected with me and solely focused on the role itself, while giving me a feel for who I was talking to get to the next stage. First, the role was in agriculture, something I was not familiar with beyond eating food. This was like being recruited as a defensive player, and then they switch you to offense, or you are a pitcher and they convert you to a catcher. You will do what needs to be done to play, but it is a whole different side of the table.

Secondly, I found it interesting that she spent most of her time discussing with whom I would be talking. The leader I would be talking to was considered high up, a skeptic, and no BS guy with an authority complex. Apparently, she didn't have a lot of success with bringing him talent, but she felt different about me. Eureka! I started to feel that this may be my first YES! All I thought was that a Fortune 100 company was in my sight and I had a challenge to convince this executive that I was his best bet.

I literally had a recruiter prepare me for the person more than the role. It felt like a teacher who likes to fail the class just to prove a point that no one knows everything, but everyone passes because the grade is based off a bell curve. Go figure! As an athlete, on your first day of classes, you get instructed to introduce yourself to your teachers so they know you play sports and may miss some classes in season, but you won't take classes lightly. You know in your head you are thinking, Well, now you have a target. It is hit or miss!

Fast forward to my first week of being recruited. I met this executive over a telephone interview. He seemed charismatic but every bit of a politician at the same time. Asked great questions and seemed genuinely to be looking for an open candidate who was local to New Jersey. My location at the time was Pennsylvania, so I knew I found a leverage point. I led with passion, focused on my behaviors and traits as an athlete, and offered to pay to come up and interview from Pennsylvania. I showed intuition, willingness, and eagerness to take the next step, while not being afraid to bet on myself. I opened my toolbox and went for it! When you see your potential "yes," take the opportunity. So, that is exactly what I did.

Right after the interview, I immediately got a call from the recruiter saying, "We did it!" I somehow got her excited about me to the point where she realized my stock value, and it went from "you" to "we." Let's call this concept the "championing" effect. Championship routine building is not only what you do day in and day out but also is paramount to get others to champion on your behalf. She immediately set up my next phone interview.

He was the leader with whom I would be working, a natural athlete and seasoned executive—smart, meticulous, and a collaborator. We spent an hour talking about scenarios and experiences. He never looked at my resume as blank because he knew what NCAA Division I athlete meant. The whole time, he wanted to see my approach and assess my coachability. I was well within my comfort zone and enjoyed the conversation. The recruiter called me a day later saying, "They want you to come to their corporate headquarters in New Jersey." I was so excited, and everything progressed so fast that I never followed up with either of them (my 101 tip).

Just think, this is corporate America, where traditionally nothing happens fast, but here I was a week and a half from a LinkedIn inquiry to two phone interviews and interview No. 3 on the books. As you know, **if someone sees your future stock value and a 100x growth, the speed and recruiting style changes. It is like a coach flying a player into the school versus the coach flying to your family so you get to meet them on a more personal level.**

I drove up to New Jersey and met with three or four people throughout the day. I stayed true to myself, but I was thankful for my MBA because they were testing both my analytical and business skill sets. My MBA became a crucial learning period for me, so what it added to my resume was worth its weight in gold. The business executive saw NCAA Division I athlete, which translated to "captain of the team, competitive, results-oriented, and disciplined." His view of chemistry major was "took a tough major, doesn't take the easy road, and would fit in our group full of engineers and chemists." And lastly, when he saw MBA, he most likely was puzzled how I had zero work experience but had still got into the program. But as part of a multinational company, he liked the bonus of my studying abroad assignment. I turned zero years of work experience into a future career at a Fortune 100 company through a LinkedIn recruiter and a drive up north. Don't ever tell me something is out of your reach. Go get it!

I bet you know the outcome: hired! From Day 1 to offer was 27 days. Upon being hired, I had never met my boss in person yet, but he hired me from what he heard and felt in his gut about me. He knew the role had never existed before, so he was looking for someone willing to make it their own, be coachable, integrate into his well-oiled team, and handle ambiguity. Be the neck, not the head, was the key! I was flexible to the direction given, was nimble when thrown scenarios, and showed stability with limited experience.

The only thing that threw me for a loop was when, within 30 minutes of receiving my offer letter, my boss asked if I had a passport. Where to? Oh, you know, just a business trip to Doha, Qatar in the Middle East. From this point forward, the pace of my life went to jetset. **The places you can go are unlimited when you lead with openness, stay curious, maintain your coachability, and are willing to adapt to new situations.** You know how to do it; just remember it may have been in a different package. Being an athlete is a business, and you do have all the tools to be a beast beyond game day. All we are doing now is putting your new package together brick by brick. You have it already. I am here to help you harness it further. As a successful rapper and entrepreneur once said, "Yesterday's price is not today's price."

Success isn't owned, it's leased,
and rent is due every day.

—J.J. Watt

Success Beyond Game Day Playbook Recap:

Your Post-Sports Afterglow: *Be the Neck, Not the Head*

1. **Go beyond setting goals** on Day 1. Sign them, and now you have a contract.
   a. Be intentional, sit down, and write out your next 20 years. Start with Year 1 and build five-year goals from there until you hit Year 20. Think about what you want and why.
   b. You will always be where you started if you do not take your first step, period.
   c. You impact lives. You are a living role model. Your goals that you are living by today could be someone's dream; never sleep on that fact.

2. **Identify the problem. Do not tolerate problems**, aka red flags.
   a. It all starts with a true open mentality and shifting from a "yes, but" to "yes, and" approach. Listen to hear; try to avoid listening to speak.
   b. Business is designed to keep the pedal down and keep you "drinking from the fire hydrant" busy. Make time to get a pulse for yourself and others. Reset often!
   c. Grow through what you go through; control the controllables.

3. **Peel back the layers** and go below the surface. Ask yourself the six whys.
   a. Understanding people (to the core), championing for people, and making necessary changes for people are all areas where the best of the best leaders exemplify the "championing" effect: from you to we!

b. Everyone has a different why, but we all have many areas of life's intersections that can lead to some of the strongest bridges and networks. Remember your network is your net worth!

4. **Lay the groundwork and foundation** with optionality and flexibility.
   a. The places you can go are unlimited when you lead with openness, stay curious, maintain your coachability, and are willing to adapt to new situations.
   b. Self-confidence, perseverance, and dedication are the key pillars of a successful athlete.
   c. Remember, more often than not, you have been there, done that; it was just in a different package.

5. **Flawless operationalization.** Game time!
   a. When you see your potential and leverage advantage, take the opportunity.

6

On and Off the Field: Go Time

Your New Day One

*I am a big believer in visualization.
I run my races mentally so that I feel
even more prepared.*

—Allyson Felix

Do you remember your rookie season? Did you feel excited but nervous, ready to go? Was your heart beating harder, deeper, faster, and louder as each second escaped? Did you have the bubble guts (if you know, you know)? Were you an ESPN *SportsCenter* recruit, or best case, a local newspaper article recruit?

Were you worried that you would not muster up to the hype and ratings? Or were you that "not highly anticipated, but we need them for well-rounded strength" recruit? Or even the potential walk-on who has nothing to lose but everything to prove? All three personas come with different insecurities, pressures, and biases. Let's debate it! Did you put your avatar on and come off "fake confident"? Were you afraid that everyone could hear and see your blood pressure rising and building intensity with each minute?

On and Off the Field: Go Time

From sports to current day, I have become quite proficient (like muscle memory) from all the experiential learning, all things avatar (aka mask or alter-ego), and my situational muscle flex. Lucky for you, I see right through your "avatar," so let's break down your barriers, leverage my learnings, and explore in this chapter where your foundational success post-sports cements itself. I told you, I am not about the settle up; I am all about the level up, so let's freaking go!

You spend years finding the sport that you will fully commit to, and when you finally make that commitment, everything else becomes noise. Were you that beast of an athlete that any sport you played, you were one of the best? Did you have your parents, coaches, and/or friends push you to pick your sport sooner rather than later? Did they corner you into a decision because "you need to play year-round," prevent an injury, benefit somehow (stock value potential), and/or take you away from your progression and focus? Oh, I know this too well! I can count on one hand who were my positive enablers and levelers. Let that sink in!

For me, softball became my focus when I was eight years old. I was a natural. Sports clicked early on for me. I fought the urge in high school to play too many sports, but volleyball was near and dear to me, too, so I made it work. I would go from practice to practice. I was on high school softball and volleyball teams and competitive travel softball teams all at the same time. I would eat in the car in between practices and then work on my homework from 7:00 p.m. to 10:00 p.m. I didn't know life outside of this schedule. Every now and then I would go to a movie with friends, but my life was all around sports. I gave up a lot of my social life as a teenager, no regrets. I most likely missed out on some great people, but I was working toward something bigger: to become an elite national athlete.

As disciplined as I was, I was not a morning person, until I got to college. I was an absolute terror in the morning. My parents used to play "rock, paper, scissors" to see who had to fight to get me up for school. I am convinced it was all about me liking the morning calm and focused "me" time outside of the everyday mundane, disciplined schedule. I sacrificed my teenage years, limited my social life, and lived against the traditional grain. From high school forward, every aspect of who I am has evolved, mentally and physically. As funny as it sounds, I lived for naps and ramen noodles (still love naps). It was my naïve version of rest (body wear and tear) and recovery (salt intake), whereas now I know the value of ice baths, sauna treatments, and balanced electrolytes (call me an evolving continuous improvement). Can you imagine if you had the knowledge and tools that you learned later on in life *earlier*? Don't you think you would have had an edge? Could you have been even better than your best?

The reason why I am illustrating my approach early on is twofold. First, it is all about understanding that as you are young, learning, and growing, you are already exposed to living a life of sacrifice, mindful of the opportunity cost and return on your investments. This is all without you knowing the true outcome, but you still push forward, full of ambition, hope, and will, building your muscle memory through practice. You may feel FOMO from time to time, but you start to shift your thinking to "Is it really worth that night out at the bar?" and "Will I pay for this at practice tomorrow?" You have more to lose than gain as an athlete so make the right choice every time!

> **First, it is all about understanding that as you are young, learning, and growing, you are already exposed to living a life of sacrifice, mindful of the opportunity cost and return on your investments.**

On and Off the Field: Go Time

Going into the unknown but predictive schedule will challenge you yet also serve opportunities for you at different levels and times. You must be ready to see what side of the field you are on and act quickly. If not, someone will take your spot, and then you become bench strength. It may get boring and feel as if you have no time, but you are building your personal stock value portfolio, knowing there is intrinsic value well ahead of the actual result. Reminder that intrinsic value relates to the measure of an asset (YOU) based on its true value, no matter the fluctuations that can occur. This behavioral and mental mind map you use, consciously and subconsciously, becomes a critical foundational blueprint before and after you cement your legacy.

Second piece of the fold is your network being your net worth and finding champions on your behalf. Not just any network, but those that get you comfortable with the uncomfortable—vulnerability, humble pie, and accountability levelers. The type of people that can change your life with one door or action. When you become successful in communicating your brand, you will get a ticket to other superior elite who can eat you for breakfast at any time (the thrill!). More often than not, you will be the "least qualified" in the room, so cherish and step into these moments where they are due, or die out in overtime.

> **Your network is your net worth and finding champions on your behalf. Not just any network, but those that get you comfortable with the uncomfortable—vulnerability, humble pie, and accountability levelers. The type of people that can change your life with one door or action.**

You need to aspire to be in this room. The conversations will change, the motivation is intoxicating, and winning is table stakes. Walk the walk when it comes to driving results. This ownership mindset will exponentially catapult and expand your success trajectory pathways. You start to piece together who is of value to your life, who holds you back, who enables you in positive and negative ways, and who adds to your future stock value without any expectation back. Be careful of those who you think are the "right network" or if you are "in the right room." You will know when you are in the room; the air is thin, and only the strong survive.

No matter if you are a highly sought-out recruit or a walk-on, the process is still the same. The journey may be different, but the process of assessing opportunity costs, ROI (return on investment), intrinsic value, and leveling up is the same (may have different scales). If you are highly recruited, nationally known, you may feel more opportunity cost in the form of not being able to go out because the eyes of the nation are on your every move, waiting for you to lose your intrinsic value. And being at the top means everyone is coming for you all the time. You must live in "no days off," and the ROI of that choice is for you to maintain at the top. Your "off day" has to be you operating at 90%, because if you are at 80%, you may just open the door for a competitor to bridge the gap. You are the target, the way for someone else to get a name, or a way to generate more "clout." It gets lonely!

If you are a walk-on, every day matters; 1% better every day is your motto. You know it will take sacrifice, and you are okay with it. Your focus is to get in the room, and once you do that, your discipline and tenacity will differentiate you. Your workouts are different; you spend painstaking amounts of time planning and redoing, over and over and over. You must be on all the time because you never know when you will get called up, get the chance, or see an opening to bridge the gap. No matter where you sit on the athletic scale, you will have different journeys, but relative process milestones must be overcome or learned to level up the bar. Key tenets (pillars) needed for success are all consistent and up to you for the taking!

You arrived! You made it to your first day with your new team. All of your initial work paid off; now what? You have a new system to learn, new teammates to gel with, new routines to form, new classes ("scholar" in scholar athlete—leverage this more), and new coaches to adapt to and "impress". **You will hear me say it often: Every day is an interview!** Will your coaches be the same as they were when they wanted you during recruiting? They should be, but remember, being an athlete is a business. You are in the business of winning championships and generating revenue for the program. You are an extension of not only a program but also an institution.

There is a hierarchy (aka levels) to the game. The president of the university is the board of directors (BOD). The athletic director is the CEO (reporting to the BOD). The assistant athletic director is the VP (reporting to the CEO). Your head coach is a director (reporting to the VP). The assistant coaches are managers (reporting the director), and you are an employee on contract! You get paid to play and produce results! If you are a walk-on, you pay to play—kind of like an internship until you get hired full-time. Your value to the enterprise in sports is your brand as an active high-performance athlete who can sell merch, fill seats, and generate more revenue through winning at the higher levels.

Don't fool yourself; there is a lot of money in this game! An interesting piece of sauce is that you may want more money, especially if you are high profile, but always remember, everyone is replaceable. There are many people who want your spot and will work at a cheaper pay rate to get in the door so they can get access to the room. Do not think for a second you are not replaceable. The sports industry (just like corporate America) is highly political and it's survival of the fittest. Early on you will learn about the pressures to win; if not, you may be playing for a new set of coaches with a whole new system, who may not share your same energy. Everyone is replaceable, so focus on what you know, find your champions and decision makers, and find ways to get access to them.

For me, Day 1 in corporate America was very much like a cheetah in the savanna (aka plains), trying to find the highest peak quickly to see the whole field and opportunity. The difference between your Day 1 athletic career and my early corporate career was that I was faced with bleak instructions on where to go, no explanation on how to get an access badge, blank dual computer screens, no laptop, no phone, cubicle seating (picture your study hall), my direct boss based in another state, global $40B highly matrixed company with thousands around but no one talking, not knowing one person, no real onboarding, the recruiter who found me not actually working for the company (outsourced), not knowing what my true job was beyond agriculture and marketing, and being a solo member from the team based in corporate. You know, "normal" Day 1.

Your Day 1 as an athlete most likely included a schedule (where to go, whom to meet, what time to be there), and a key contact for your team. You may have felt blind, but you were well spoken for on your Day 1. I can pretty much bet your onboarding was streamlined point to point (assuming you were on scholarship). My class schedule was already populated when I had arrived, and my books were literally packed for me to pick up! This was always a sore subject for the broader student body!

> **You may have felt blind, but you were well spoken for on your Day 1.**

Between the sweats and the side entrance we had as athletes, we were always a target.

On and Off the Field: Go Time

As a corporate employee I needed self-starter behavior and handle ambiguity. My heartbeat was increasing second by second with my pulse feeling faster and shorter. All I needed to do was breathe, but I didn't. Picture me in a stiff, uncomfortable two-piece suit, overdressed versus the majority. Who did I think I was?

In these moments, you have a choice on how you will respond despite that feeling of "What the heck did I sign up for?" coupled with "Grow through what you go through."

Picture me sitting in a cubicle for the first five days with no laptop, barely talking to anyone, chatter around questioning if I was a former athlete, three 300-page marketing reports, and a literal plane ticket to Doha, Qatar.

Success Beyond Game Day

Not to forget my living situation the first 30 days when I moved from Pittsburgh. I had a packed-full Mustang and an Airbnb lake house basement apartment situated in the outskirts of New Jersey until I found my ultimate spot in Hoboken. No lie, it was rough pickings! If anyone had robbed my car, they would have taken all I owned at the time. All I kept thinking about was "Do not be naïve, learn to appropriately dress, and understand where I am going and what I need to know to be effective at work." My goal was: Do not wing this Middle East trip. To ground you, at this point in my life, I had been to the Bahamas and Western Europe.

I was the type of professional who was ahead of the game, had an urgency to get things done, and was structured. However, anything to do with making my personal self have an easier go at it was just not even an option or area where I would learn from my past mistakes. I was last-minute on everything personally. This only impacted myself and no one else so I never saw the issue. Go figure! My people pleaser skills crippled my ability to focus on efficiencies for myself. I could have been driven by getting into a new routine, but I somehow was convinced that I didn't need any help (oh, the lies!). I was focused on making sure my boss (the coach) and organization knew I was worth the time, that I got myself acclimated and solid. This was classic "working harder, not smarter!" It's ridiculous to write about, but I promised to be granular. Pride and ego can fuel you in positive ways, but in my case, it weighed me down. This was an important behavioral insight that took years to peel back as I was developing as a corporate leader.

> **I was the type of professional who was ahead of the game, had an urgency to get things done, and was structured.**

So, **now you can picture the "drinking from the fire hydrant" and the absolute disarray of my initial week in corporate America. I got through it, though! Remember, when you feel you are in the thick of the storm, keep walking.** Do you really want to stop in the rain, or do you want to get to the other side where the calm is after the storm? I chose to keep walking, learn, and feel all the feels on this journey. It is like the pain you get when pushing your physical limits in a workout; most of the time, it is mentally getting through it. Mentally I would tell myself that the "pain" would end in a finite amount of time. This mentality got me through the hardest workouts of my life! I reapplied this mental focus to my first work week.

Day 7 of my corporate career was flying out of Newark airport, connecting in Washington Dulles airport, with a roundtrip ticket to Doha, Qatar, and finally meeting my direct boss for the first time. Can you imagine just talking to your coach on the phone and never meeting them until you are headed on a global trip to a big conference with limited knowledge? I didn't know what he looked like, so connecting with him was difficult. To add to the awkwardness, he texted me where he was, I found him, and he was on a conference call when I showed up. So, I sat there, trying not to stare, but impatiently waiting to assess our compatibility.

Success Beyond Game Day

I remembered thinking in the phone interview how great he was, easy to talk to, but would he be the same as when he recruited me? I took the three 300-page reports out and began studying them like I was in finals. I don't even really think I was reading as much as trying to fill the void. He got off the phone, and his first words were awesome: "I am so sorry I couldn't get you upgraded. With the last-minute nine-hour flight, I wanted to try to make you comfortable." He was on a conference call but also trying to get me upgraded at the same time. He was genuinely trying to make me as comfortable as possible and emotionally astute of the overall situation. By the way, he had never been to the Middle East, so we shared an unknowingness ahead that we would tackle together.

With recruiting these days, you may indeed have had this happen, relative to not meeting face-to-face, but you do know why you are going to the program (or you really should). Be prepared to handle ambiguity with a level head and humble sincerity because you may come in as a shortstop and end up a catcher. Adapt, be resilient, bridge the gap, narrow the learning curve, and go to work. You may transfer to a new department in the future or get traded to another team or spinoff from the company and have to learn a new system quickly; deal with it! Embrace and align, assess and identify, lay the groundwork and foundation, and execute.

Fast forward to arriving in Qatar, thrown into the "learn by fire" (pun intended), and the output resulted in handling the challenge, bonding with my new leader (who no longer just felt like a boss), and spearheading my inner beast mode to truly want to climb the ladder.

On and Off the Field: Go Time

The first true leader (will call him MH) whom I ever had the privilege to work for is still an important mentor to me. He is a huge part of the reason I am the way I am. He helped establish the right materials and support that I needed to build my foundational base. He helped me pour the cement. MH is rare and so appreciated by me. If I can be half of who he is as a leader, I will make a huge impact on many lives. I am hoping yours is one of them!

I would do anything for MH because he took me under his wing and then gave me creative freedom to fail fast and experience new opportunities. He was and still is the real deal! I consider MH family! As highlighted, your foundational blueprint truly needs a strong network that drives your net worth (stock value). Finding champions on your behalf who help mentor you so you don't work harder, but rather work smarter, is paramount to the start of your success's longevity. They will get you comfortable with the uncomfortable marathon; be a master sponge and go above and beyond for your accountability levelers. When you can have access to these types of people, they can change your life. MH changed mine!

Success Beyond Game Day

As we progress through your journey, let's drill down on how to leverage my experiences and find the applicability to your specific goals. Your journey is and will be exciting, full of ups and downs. You will start to understand that establishing a championship routine requires mentors and coaches who help guide your greatness. When you take a few critical learning areas from this whole entire book, this lesson is one of the most important! When you find your champions, you go above and beyond 150% of the time, period. You make it known that their time is valuable, and you work tirelessly to utilize your coachability building block to the fullest. I call the next couple of lessons the "sponge season." You will walk into new chapters of life and rooms full of different lessons, so let's get you equipped to recognize, leverage, and take action while staying true to those who helped prop you up to get there.

> Your journey is and will be exciting, full of ups and downs. You will start to understand that establishing a championship routine requires mentors and coaches who help guide your greatness. When you take a few critical learning areas from this whole entire book, this lesson is one of the most important!

Let's get it! Next stop, "Athletes Are the Best Bet." Get ready to join the debate!

Success Beyond Game Day Playbook Recap:

On and Off the Field: Go Time: *First Day of Business*

1. **Go beyond setting goals** on Day 1. Sign them, and now you have a contract.
   a. Let your youthful yearning for learning and growing curiosity lead you out of the gate.
   b. You already know a life of sacrifice, opportunity costs, and return on your investments; just reframe and reapply to the world of business.
   c. When you shift from "humble pie" to "sponge" season, you know you are right where you need to be. Progress is a beautiful thing! Work smarter, not harder.

2. **Identify the problem. Do not tolerate problems**, aka red flags.
   a. Embrace and align, assess, and identify; you can't lay down the foundation without truly understanding the issue and your respective skill set at hand.
   b. Adapt, be resilient, bridge the gap, narrow the learning curve, and go to work.
   c. Learning a new system quickly will be a differentiator; allow yourself to transition from feeling overwhelmed to slowing the game down and shortening the window to drive results.

3. **Peel back the layers** and go below the surface. Ask yourself the six whys.
   a. Your journey is and will be exciting, full of ups and downs; establishing a championship routine requires mentors and coaches who help guide your greatness.

b. Get out of your own way. No one is going to give you a medal if you don't ask for help. Get over the ego and pride of not being the best in every aspect of business, sports, and life.
   c. The most successful people have a team and mentors helping to guide them to the promised land of success. Why do you think you are different? Tap in!

4. **Lay the groundwork and foundation** with optionality and flexibility.

   a. Finding champions on your behalf who help mentor you so you don't work harder is paramount to the start of your success's longevity. Let others help pour your foundational cement with you!
   b. There is no ONE way to be successful. Stop looking for a distinct list of "If you do 1, 2, and 3, you will be the top of your game." Your game plan is unique to you. Aim to use the different tools to get your base sturdy first!

5. **Flawless operationalization.** Game time!

7

Athletes Are THE Best Bet, Period

Solidifying Your Valuable Stock Position

It isn't the mountains ahead to climb that wear you out; it's the pebble in your shoe.

—Muhammad Ali

Who are you beyond sports? I am asking, "Who are you to the core?" Challenge yourself, go beyond surface-level scratching, and dig into what truly drives you. Leave behind what others may think and enter exploring *you* and what makes you *you*! What is important to who you are today and in the future? You may need to put the book down and jot it out to the left. Think! Be curious! Be intentional! Have a thoughtful debate with yourself. I am pushing you to be open-minded and limitless to your today, tomorrow, and future potential!

After you think through it, practice expressing out loud "who you are" and "why you matter." Fumble over your delivery and master crafting your brand value proposition. Think of a brand value proposition as your game day strategy that is exemplified through a single statement that embodies who you are, what you stand for, your capabilities, and why it matters to others. No big deal, just your whole life's work in a single sentence—simple, right?

Here is your chance (in safe waters) to really think about it. If you skip this first opportunity to drill down and skim through "all things you," just know, you will always be where you started. If you can't spend the productive time for you, now, in a moment of intentional selfishness, then how can you do anything 150% in life? **How you do anything is how you do everything. I am here to coach you up, but you must want to be here. Your choice.** I can bring you to the water and teach you ways to capture the water, but you must drink the water to survive. It is time to hit this head-on! Remember when I mentioned to get ready to get comfortable with being uncomfortable?

Welcome! You have arrived at the start of what every day from here requires. It is all about being intentional and solidifying your personal and professional stock value. Thus far, we have dabbled in the "what," "how," and "why" this journey requires what it does. Now it is time to pierce beyond the surface-level concepts. Think about when you jump into cold water. It is a perfect mix of the mental rationalization of knowing the ice-cold pierce is ahead and the physical numb feeling that overtakes you upon impact. It becomes hard-to-breathe coupled with goosebump welts and a hot/cold sensation all over your body, but you still make the decision to descend into the water. In this moment, when your body first touches the surface of water (Kaboom/Slam/Pow/Smack), it is like cement, like hitting a sturdy brick wall head-on. That short pain on impact subsides as you break the surface area.

Why do you think a belly flop sounds excruciating? The lucky person comes head-to-head with a brick-wall slam all at once, a deer-caught-in-headlights feeling, a body shock impact like hypothermia, a slow rise to get back to the surface while craving oxygen, and a radiant red afterglow (aka the trophy). As a science nerd, I felt compelled to give you a science visualization on what I am driving you toward: breaking through the surface level. So many lessons in this example!

Success Beyond Game Day

To be successful in your "red afterglow" requires:

More comfortable

1. Knowing who you are (start here first and establish what you will or will not embark upon)

2. Being hyper-aware and disciplined to what matters to you and why (your filter)

3. Aligning with the right crew: coaches, mentors, friends, and family (establishing your influencers and eliminating your limiters—your network is your net worth)

4. Knowing this is a marathon, not a sprint (no procrastination, just life/goal milestones)

5. Letting your mental space go wild and work to overcome the crippling effect of practice and recentering (learn, "feel all the feels," and reframe your mindset)

6. Taking the plunge, knowing it may be tough on impact at the start, but below the surface is fluidity and limitless possibilities

7. Getting back in the boat, repeating the fall, feeling the impact (now you know the feeling), and then learning how to dive in differently to break the surface (fail fast, learn, and adapt)

8. Evolving, with every jump, as does your brand; leveraging it (hone in on continuous improvements to your brand, practice talking about it, assess if you have new filters, and elevate your position)

More uncomfortable

At this point, you chose to get into the boat with the information presented thus far. I am here to help you navigate out of the dock with no wake (no major waves) and into the start of open waters. I am looking for you to see, feel, and hear how the controls work so you can drive your boat where you want it to go. We are partnering together to get you prepared and ready for the open water. You will have the sticks and will determine who is allowed on the boat, how fast or slow we go, and when and where we anchor.

You are the captain. Like any new skill, it takes time, but you are a high-performing athlete, so you are built differently. You can deal and execute under tough conditions with each day adding to your productive mastery of "drinking from the fire hydrant" mixed with "learning by fire." We get it done and make it happen. Elite athletes live every day with every interaction being an interview (or you should be). You assess thousands of opportunities while testing new physical and mental boundaries regularly. You have new systems put upon you and new teammates each year. You can manage everything from a team of seasoned players to a whole new team filled with rookies. You flawlessly interact with different types of personalities and skill sets of team members, and you learn fast if you don't see the glue drying together. You have won and lost. You deal with critics and fans who forget you are human from time to time. You must be every bit of a scholar athlete on and off the field. You, as an elite athlete, must wear multiple hats and produce results. Just another day at the office!

> **We get it done and make it happen. Elite athletes live every day with every interaction being an interview (or you should be).**

Out of the gate, you may feel uneasy or overwhelmed inside, but you push through and put on your avatar (alter ego). You start to realize your network is on the boat. You can leverage your network when you need help, heed advice when you need a sounding board, and, as ever, learn as you go with support next to you. You must shift your mentality from "working hard to get to a comfortable state" to more of "test to fail" every day. Once you hit comfortable, you already need your next path toward elevation. It is not easy, but it is well within your abilities to achieve. When the game slows down because you see everything clearer, that is when you know you need to notch it up!

You drive the boat, and you will determine the speed. The decisions on direction and pace that you make now will have a lasting impact, so my advice for you at this moment is to proceed with the mindset of "If you are not first, you are last." Show urgency to get things done, but don't confuse that with speed. All I am saying is, don't have an "off day" early on because how you do anything is how you do everything.

Don't give yourself permission to slack off; keep the throttle down. Upon anchoring at your first stop, the water should look fairly calm. Remember, do not anchor in the heart of a storm; get through it before you stop. Grow through what you go through, good or bad. Anchored learning is critical to grounding your base, so now that we have aligned on core "afterglow" tenets, from this point forward, we are about the BUILD and plunge into action!

Now we pivot to writing out your contract, although you know it as a list of goals. **Sounds fancy and fluffy, but it is merely about converting your dreams and beliefs into goals and vision with timelines. Emphasis on timelines and conversion.** Some of your programs and organizations will have tools in place already, so let's tap into them if you have a good starting point. No need to recreate the wheel here! Work smarter, not harder. A common example that I have seen universally used is SMART goals. It's a great tool to add structure to your goals and vision! I want to take it up a notch, though.

Athletes Are THE Best Bet, Period

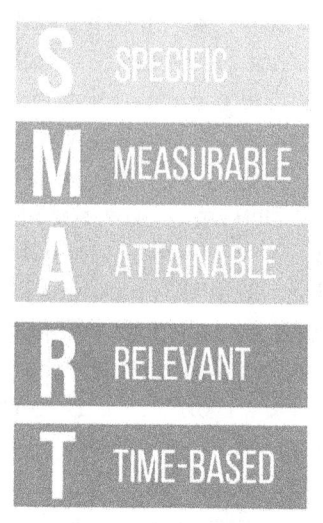

There are many fantastic tools and models that can help you focus on targeted areas of your life that drive action, where you can learn from and hold yourself accountable to complete within a certain period. I have found SMART goals are quite helpful for many people. On the other hand, many of these streamlined tools (one size fits all) keep you at surface level and within your comfortable range (with periods of challenge). For me, as an athlete fueled for elevation with a hyper-focus on being No. 1 in every aspect of my life, these tools didn't seem to fit my full needs. Why?

Think about it; I have spent my whole life competing and getting better every day. As I progressed and got promoted every 6-12 months in the corporate world, I realized how cheap the company got my stock. Think about if you had invested $10,000 in 2016 in Bitcoin when it was about $450. The value you would have today in bitcoin would be over $900,000. Just think, if you only had invested $1,000 in Bitcoin in 2016 you would have netted over $90,000 now (not too bad). I get it: Who knew cryptocurrency would get here? But that is the way it works. You are either the innovator, early adopter, neutral position (not leaning one way, but not needing to be first), or like most of the general mass population, going to "wait and see" as the world moves on to the next evolution of currency exchange! Do your due diligence, but take a plunge in every now and then (small scale)!

Source: Publicly traded data utilized by the Coinbase Platform

Or a more traditional example, investing in Amazon. If you had invested in Amazon in January 2016 for $10,000 (~17 shares), then your value today (after ~6 years) would be +$45,000.

Athletes Are THE Best Bet, Period

Amazon

I illustrated the early years of Bitcoin and Amazon because this is how I felt when corporate America threw tens of thousands at me each year along with the promotions. On the surface, it looked great. My salary grew greater than inflation (bottom line is, I was making more money even if the value of money was going down), but when they throw you a performance bonus so easily, you know they got you for cheap. Let this be a lesson. I am pushing you to lay this out now rather than later! **Know your brand value proposition, lay out critical milestones, and once you hit them, go for an increase during an off-cycle. You will never get what you don't ask for!** Do not wait for your mid-year or full-year performance review. Discussions around compensation and bonuses happen way before the reviews, so go after it! This is a big miss on my part early on!

Never forget, your likeability can get you a champion on your behalf, mentors, and some one-on-ones with decision-makers, but your results and brand get you in the room. Executives (or coaches) may like you, and you may be in the top 1% talent pool, but you could be paid lower than a "middle of the pack" employee (teammate) if you don't smarten up. Think about that. Does that fire you up? It fired me up because this was a problem area that I tolerated. It was a problem that I never addressed until later on! To give you a feel, I negotiated multi-million-dollar contracts and managed hundreds of millions of dollars for the company, yet I never negotiated my performance bonus level. I have been at the same bonus level since 2017, despite having brought in millions! How does that work? Shame on me for tolerating that! Thankfully, I wised up on investing!

I was a year into my newly promoted role, having moved from being an analyst to being the marketing manager (acting as a senior manager/director on projects). At this point, at the age of 26, I had had three pay increases, double-digit bonuses, been promoted a few times, and traveled to 50% of the US, 5% of Western Europe, and 1% of South America. Life was moving at a good speed (on the surface level), but I had so much more to give (below the surface)! I felt I had a runway and needed to make sure it was known that I was ready to captain at any time. My mentality started to shift. All I would think about was the who, what, why, how, and the situational and emotional intelligence needed to be called up to the majors. Remember, up to this point, my goals in life were all tied to playing at the highest levels. It was a great goal, but too broad and singular! It was what I was working with at the time, early on, but deep down I knew there was more to me than accolades and getting to the top.

I started asking about learning opportunities for executive presence techniques and communication seminars. My curiosity and eagerness, being vouched for by key leaders, and having sponge like coachability led to me to getting my first chance at rubbing elbows with the CMO, SVPs, and directors. I was championed by my direct boss, MH, to be included in the Marketing Best Bet program. This was a big deal! I had access to different business executives, top-notch leaders, and up-and-coming peers who were levelers in the marketing space. I was in the right room, like you will be, and on paper the most "inexperienced!" I thrived in these moments, and so will you! I was in the room based upon my hard work, ambition, impact results, and future merit. My stock was now headed toward an "IPO" (initial public offering in the stock market). Being in the top 10% wasn't good enough; I wanted to find a way to be in the top 1%. **I learned about key marketing principles and tools, but it all came down to brand positioning, marketability on BOTH sides of the table, proper planning, and unwavering, highly stretched goals to drive your results. Think about that!**

Have you ever had a rude awakening that made you question everything you have ever done or known? What I realized quickly was I didn't have goals that were tied to my true mission: being No. 1 in all aspects of my life. They were tied to the today, tomorrow, and year, but never around the medium-, long-term, or stretch. Take a serious moment and ask yourself, do you have real goals that you can confidently speak to today? Are your goals easily achievable? Do any of them make you uncomfortable? Do you have anything tied to anything for over four years? Think about it; you can be an active NCAA athlete for four years (sometimes five to six years if redshirted) or a professional player for maybe five to eight years depending on the sport and position. You spend many years after you "retire" in other endeavors and business relationships. Don't you think setting your intention and goals around who you are and what is important to you becomes ever more important?

I was shocked at how tied mine were to actions and results that I knew I could hit within a few months, not stretch goals at all! How was that possible? I loved failing (I still do)! My goals were broad and singular, but everyone else who saw them thought they were ambitious. As athletes, you know that we are built different. We do not think or process things the same, and at times, it feels lonely knowing no one truly understands your obsessive drive toward excellence.

Your intention sets your motion, and your innate drive meticulously lays out how you can accomplish it. Do not set yourself up for the bare minimum needed to hit a "goal" that isn't a goal. Have a passion for failing fast because that means you are growing. It means you are touching the surface and finding ways to dive in with constant pressure! Be careful of those around you and your environment because that can rub off on you or close the gap in the wrong way. Do you really want to be the No. 1 team that plays down to the No. 50 team and loses? Setting only attainable goals and lackluster grit is exactly the same thing as playing down to your competition.

Have a passion for failing fast because that means you are growing. It means you are touching the surface and finding ways to dive in with constant pressure!

Learn from my shortsightedness and address problems early on. Turn problems into opportunities. Take your goals seriously because you have one lifetime to aspire to greatness. Challenge yourself to go from short-sighted, singular goals to more written-down contract goals with incentives and penalties. From 2013 forward, over 80% of my goals have been difficult to achieve. If I do not operate at 150% each day, I will not achieve my goals, period. Just like me, you are built different, so that means you need to take different approaches. I apply many concepts, but I am not afraid to tweak and challenge the "one size fits all" mentality. I built a model that leverages many great tools out there. It isn't about reinventing the wheel but adapting and evolving so you can get 1% better every day.

Now let's drill down on your contract. **Write down three to four goals in present tense with powerful intentions and**

dates. Next to each goal date, add a section that says "when I hit this goal," and list a reward. Of course, you will need to fully fill this out and sign at the bottom. Frame it where you can see it every day. If you can't do this, how do you expect to aspire to success, let alone wealth? Leave no detail or rock unturned. Start with the basics, incorporate the stretch target, and build the championship routine.

Please see a sample on the next page. You may copy it and use it for your Contract, or just write it in this book.

Success Beyond Game Day

Name:

GOAL 1   Date

_____
_____

When I hit this goal:
_____

GOAL 2   Date

_____
_____

When I hit this goal:
_____

GOAL 3   Date

_____
_____

When I hit this goal:
_____

GOAL 4   Date

_____
_____

When I hit this goal:
_____
_____

Goals Section: Start here before you build out your SMART goals (with stretch!)
[Your Name and Date]:
Start with all things you! You are the brand!

- Who are you to the core? **Why?**
- What makes you comfortable? **Why?**
- What makes you uncomfortable? **Why?**
- What drives you? **Why?**
- Where do you want to be in 2,5,10,15+ years? **Why?**
- What does success look like to you? **Why?**

Learn about yourself! Then work on goals! Here are some examples to get you started. Drop the "I" if you need to but keep the present tense!

I drive ___	I manage ___	I learn ___	I establish ___
I lead ___	I own ___	I acquire ___	I action ___
I champion ___	I reach ___	I develop ___	I close ___
I create ___	I set up ___	I promote ___	I execute ___

Do not forget to add "by when" at the end of each of them! Challenge yourself! Remember, do not do tomorrow what you can do today! Stay present!

Rewards Section (Next to your goals):

- When I hit goal #1: Reward yourself with something small you have always wanted.
    - Examples: full day to do whatever you want to do, sleep in, buy ice cream

- When I hit goal #2: Reward someone in your family with something small.
    - Examples: buy them dinner, phone call catching up, planned time to hang
- When I hit goal #3: Reward a mentor, coach, or friend with something small.
    - Examples: buy them dinner, planned time to hang, support their cause
- When I hit goal #4: Reward yourself with something bigger.
    - Example: go on a trip by yourself, buy a pair of shoes, take a full day off
- When I accomplish all goals: Reward yourself and others at the same time.
    - Example: day trip, movie together, cook dinner for everyone

You are going to start to understand that creating meaningful goals takes time. Your insight and knowing who you are and where you want to go drives this—thus, the method to my madness in asking you the same question in almost every chapter so far. Who are you beyond sports? Be prepared for me to ask you face-to-face in the future. We are in this together.

Set your goals, make them hard, write them down, set a date, reward yourself and others along the way, and set higher bars going forward. Rewarding yourself and others are important. Celebrate your roses, but don't dwell. Do not

> **Set your goals, make them hard, write them down, set a date, reward yourself and others along the way, and set higher bars going forward.**

wait for the end of the year to set goals. As new opportunities pop up, add amendments with new goals to your contracts.

Write your goals down, not type them—emphasis on WRITE THEM. I do not care if you write them on an iPad, within this book, or on a notepad, but the act of writing them down is important. **You are creating a contract with yourself. This is the first of many to come.** When I come to your school and chop it up with you and your team, we will explore how the human brain retains information. I learned so much from knowing how the human brain is wired. It can give you a leg up and foresight into why others do what they do! I will enlist experts to illustrate how the combination of visual, auditory, and sensory impacts you and your biases along with the differences between men and women and athletes versus non-athletes. There are many good studies out there, and I am convinced so much more is needed to shed light on how athletes' brains evolve and handle trauma (especially in contact sports). Write your goals down because you see yourself writing it. Saying it out loud makes you hear it, and the act of writing it make you feel its seriousness. **Print it out and put it in a frame where you see it every day. I have my goals in three places: my office, my bag when I travel, and on my nightstand.**

Now that you spent time on your goals, let's pick up the pace. What holds you back from getting to where you want to go? Who holds you back? Your Day 1s are the first to be assessed; deal with it! I am here to help you address and assess (not judge) what fits and what does not fit in your life of success. You need to let go of any and all dead weight. I am talking about anything that is not aiding in your purpose-driven mission. If you do not know what your mission is, go back to the top and reflect, jot it down, or call me!

Sometimes it will get lonely living a life of excellence, but trust me, it is so worth the sacrifice. It is like winning the national title, Super Bowl, and Olympics over and over again! I told you, I am investing in YOU! Start learning to invest in yourself! I am asking tough and extremely relevant questions required to progress further through this playbook.

Start before you are ready! Be open-minded through this journey and know that you are not alone. You are working toward surviving in the thin air where the best of the best reside. DO NOT START SOMETHING AND NOT FINISH IT! Are you going to do just one of your four sets? No, you are going to do all four sets and come back tomorrow and do four sets plus added some cardio. This is the marathon, not a darn sprint, so listen, absorb, and come run with me. Without pausing, reflecting, and assessing who you are and why you matter, you will go on a hamster-wheel journey with moments of gasping for air.

Follow my lead, and you will be successful. Be humble and vulnerable when addressing areas in your life where you tolerate problems. Understand where your base skill set is versus where you want it to be. Find yourself a team of levelers who may not have the same purpose but have the same unwavering drive. And hone your ability to build yourself from the ground up with creativity and ambiguity. I am going to ask you yet again, "Who are you beyond sports?" I am interested in learning more. You have five minutes—GO!

[PAUSE MOMENT!]
Don't waste these intentional moments to practice,
even if it is just you in the mirror!

Trust the process. You can do more than you think you can. How about I show you how I got called up to the majors and was asked to find $10B worth of opportunities in five weeks? I don't dish what I do not practice, bet! I am sure you

Athletes Are THE Best Bet, Period

are starting to get a feel for my style, so what do you think the outcome of that endeavor was?

Yeah, you are right: PURE SUCCESS DRIVEN BY A LOT OF FAST FAILURES!

Being an athlete is a business. You are built different. You know how to win. You take on many things at one time. You sacrifice to make things happen. You are the energy that moves people to a common purpose daily. You have a toolbox that can't be bought. You are unique, rare, and purpose-driven. You are a best bet in any form needed.

I show up every day; what about you?

LET'S GO!

The only person who can stop you from reaching your goals is you.

—Jackie Joyner-Kersee

Success Beyond Game Day Playbook Recap:

Athletes are THE Best Bet, Period: *Solidifying Your Valuable Stock Position*

1. **Go beyond setting goals** on Day 1. Sign them, and now you have a contract.
   a. Leverage SMART concepts; take it a step further and add more stretch goals, with present tense, powerful intentions, and dates. Add a "when I hit this goal" section (reward yourself and others!). Sign your contract!
   b. With structure comes the right view of where you are and the value you bring. Turn problems to opportunities.
   c. You will never go where you want to go without taking the first step. Who cares if it is steep?
2. **Identify the problem. Do not tolerate problems**, aka red flags.
   a. Consistent success is driven by multiple fast failures. Embrace this! When you fail, you try, and you do not tolerate.
   b. Trust the process. You can do more than you think you can. Apply how you approach a PR in the weight room or during competition, and break through the mental wall in life post sports.
   c. Understand where your base skill set is versus where you want it to be. Find yourself a team of levelers who add to your toolbox (big facts right here!).

3. **Peel back the layers** and go below the surface. Ask yourself the six whys. (Yes, literally ask yourself "why" six times. Trust me on this!)
    a. Get away from trying to not miserably fail. Oh, to the contrary, FAIL OFTEN AND FAIL FAST!
    b. If you fail at the same thing repeatedly, ask yourself why 6x. There is something below the surface that is preventing you from taking the lesson. Address it early and often. We don't repeat the same thing over and over unless it is a championship win, period!
    c. Time is money, so learn how to leverage your best strengths and then team up with others who are better in certain areas of the game so you can get where you need to go faster. Smarter, not harder!

4. **Lay the groundwork and foundation** with optionality and flexibility.
    a. You have a toolbox that can't be bought. You are unique, rare, and purpose-driven. You are a best bet in any form needed. Start leveraging this!
    b. Start before you are ready!
    c. You don't always have to be the one who has all of the skills 100% nailed down to execute—almost impossible!
    d. Extract more value by taking the extra step, going off cycle, and asking for what you want! Prepare for this conversation, and you will be pleasantly surprised.

5. **Flawless operationalization.** Game time!

8

The $10 Billion Project in 5 Weeks

Fail Fast to Learn Fast and Slow the Game Down

If something stands between you and your success, move it. Never be denied.

—Dwayne "The Rock" Johnson

Now you should be starting to see why we, as athletes, are THE "Marketing Best Bet." What do you do when your success signs you up for a $10B assignment due in five weeks with a political chess game unfolding? Where every day you feel the pressure of that game or match and that "beast mode" was your only option? Where you have 50% wanting you to win and the other 50% hoping you fail so they can say, "I told you so"? Let's be clear: Every day is an interview, an elevator pitch, an opportunity to drive your brand.

> **Let's be clear: Every day is an interview, an elevator pitch, an opportunity to drive your brand.**

This assignment was a career changer or ender scenario. Synonymous with getting first-team all-conference/

All-American or getting released from the starting lineup/team. A group of individuals who barely know you nominate you and vote on your performance as if they have seen more than film. It is all about marketability and positioning; do not forget this!

The start of this project consisted of a literal blank sheet of paper, a dedicated war room, six members, and a five-week timeclock. The goal was to create a full cohesive cross-enterprise strategy that aligned with a key macrotrend (global trends) while further bolstering our organic (internal expansion: pipeline, new products, more output) position and opening the doors for intentional technology acquisition that could get us there faster. Imagine Day 1 for me, the most junior person (total of three years of work experience) in a room full of Kobes, Jordans, Muhammed Alis, Derek Jeters, and Lionel Messis. The game felt fast, like drinking from a fire hydrant, but I tapped into that inner athlete building block, "beast mode." In that moment I knew was in the right room! I was part of the promise to Wall Street to MAKE IT HAPPEN! But what happens when you get asked to prove why it won't work just as much as how you can make it work? Is there enough time for this?

As high-performing athletes, if we aren't first, we are last, period. Only the top 1-2% can handle the pressure, navigate with the pace, establish trust with the "always 'no' first, risk-averse" group, and get more senior individuals to fight over being a part of the outcome. **Knowing people's WHYS is what makes a phenomenal leader, and understanding there is a role for everyone to play will be your differentiator.** Think about it like this: You get recruited by a team based upon your individual skill set and get a system placed on you without any say on who joins, and you as part of the team are expected to perform at the highest level.

Success Beyond Game Day

There are three outcomes when faced with your "getting called up to the big leagues" day. My favorite: lean all the way in, step up, and run right to it. This is the archetype of the Athlete Advantage and in my estimation represents the top 2%. The second outcome is "say yes but stay in the back" type, where it is all show, no value. I am sure we can agree, based on your daily experiences with others, this group represents the majority, +90%. The ones who stay close long enough to tap in later when you have won and boldly remind you "they were your Day 1s." And lastly, the third outcome is shown by those who shy away and say no without saying no. Believe it or not, there is a place for these types of people, too, in the future.

As you can imagine, I leaned all the way in, ran right to the opportunity, and was signed up for a $10B—yes, with a "B," not an "M"—project. (Sidebar: $1 Billion is equivalent to spending over $10K a day for +200 years and having change left over. Check my numbers, I dare you!) No big deal, I was dealing with $10 Billion! In fact, not only was I dealing with this massive target pipeline under a time crunch, but I was also reconciling the corporate chess game unfolding with the most senior executives. It was a race to the CEO chair coupled with the chase toward a global macrotrend. Think of a macrotrend as a major shift in direction on a large scale that impacts the globe. You may hear others talk about phenomena, but let's keep it simple. Some of the most well-known macrotrends to this day are demographics (aging and urbanization), energy, technology (automation), environment (food and water security), governance, and sustainability. We were focused on the environmental side of things.

For a solid 1.5 weeks, we moved vertically and horizontally across different business units and segments with extremely different people and cultures. Yes, the real peeled-back view of corporate America filled with the greatest minds and pride, with different biases and ownership mindsets. I am not even going to discuss the fact that I was about 25 years old with this in my lap! In my mind, age is nothing but a number!

> Yes, the real peeled-back view of corporate America filled with the greatest minds and pride, with different biases and ownership mindsets.

From the enterprise CEO to the segment CEO, general managers, and business technology marketing leads, the team had to granularly understand where base state was and build from there. This didn't come without bumps. Many thought we were infringing on their life's work and career. A good way to think about the situation was managing the egos of multiple A Teams. They all had elite skills, so much so that we had to adapt and lead with a different guiding principle set compared to when working with a team of rookies. It is the difference between high school sports and NCAA and ultimately pro level. The game is faster at each stage when you start. The players in the room become more elite, and they see the game differently, are more intentional, and are less reactive based off their experiential learning.

After two weeks and 20-hour days, taking the train home to NYC was a highlight. Some nights I slept at work, showered at the gym, and started each new day with a blank sheet of paper and my disciplined consistency. This became less about me and more about showing others how much I wanted to see their life's work at the front. I became the ultimate teammate, the culmination of a real problem identifier, root cause aficionado, and blueprint architect, by merely "listening to hear, not listening to speak." As I retrospectively look back and leverage the great teachings of Dr. Steve L. Robbins,[3] I recognize that staying curious and understanding people's biases helped guide my mental mapping through a lot of the brick walls.

1. What journey did they walk?
2. What journey did I walk?
3. Why am I right?

Four weeks in, still operating with little sleep, but making major progress. I will keep it real: Weeks 2 through 3, we still fought with multiple businesses' cultural differences, a lot of thoughtful and higher-decibel debates, some no-shows (but we covered them), and a lot of critics! **The team never wavered, and my motto to every person I talked to was "trust the process" and I would not let them down. I would be doing you a disservice if I didn't let you know that I learned the most about people during the side conversations.**

Some days I was called names, and some days I was apologized to by some of the most brilliant minds. I showed empathy and understanding, even when I didn't feel I had any. Why? Because I knew how to win. **In order to win, you** put your pride to the side and figure it out. You take the extra step no one else would. Not because you had to, but because you want to. After some of the name calling got out of the way, we went from forcing a strategy to partnering and understanding, while the train was really starting to take off!

We utilized every tool to illustrate the plan; every consultant agency would be proud! The team came up with solutions that all benefited from, leveraging many people's career work, and targeted key macrotrends for long runway growth, while proving both the enterprise CEO and segment CEO were right! Should I end this chapter with "checkmate" yet? I wish! This was only the beginning. It took four of our five weeks to make substantial progress! I went from a rookie to experienced leader while being humble in every room I walked into. Every interaction was an interview in my mind!

I continued to get into the most senior rooms through this project. I was constantly being challenged to see if I would be able to step up as the rookie or just fall flat. It became a fun game for the senior executives in my mind. See how much coaching and discipline she has and how she doesn't over-speak nor let her passion and impulsive young career headspace get the best of her. Well, the one thing I learned as a high-performing athlete was do the work, become the expert, prepare properly, and do not give anyone a reason to question that.

> When asked a tough question, I fought every urge to burst out the answer, but rather looked at the captain in the room and would intentionally say, "Permission to speak?"

When asked a tough question, I fought every urge to burst out the answer, but rather looked at the captain in the room and would intentionally say, "Permission to speak?" Even when they asked me the question directly, I would always start off with that line. I am sure none of them would remember that, but I sure do!

As highlighted earlier, I would "listen to hear, not listen to speak." This still is a practice area for me that I fail all the time at!

To give you a feel of how granular I got, I would write down every question by every single senior executive in every meeting. I became proficient in what was interesting to them and their expectations, and I armed myself with proper preparation for every moment ahead. Little did people realize the magnitude of what I did there. I showed respect, discipline, intention, situational leadership, and coachability. It wasn't a façade; it was real-time learning and adapting quickly, like we do in overtime or extra innings or penalty kicks! I fought my inner impulsive, passionate self daily! The game started to slow down, just like it did for you as you progressed in your collegiate sports career, and in some cases professionally. Mission complete.

Next order of business was to put all the pieces together with the team into a cohesive strategy with clear recommendations and a thorough organizational integration plan. Being concise and integrating were not my bread and butter, so I had to adapt on this one! Remember the ultimate goal from Day 1: Create a full cohesive cross-enterprise strategy that aligned with a key macrotrend while further bolstering our organic position and opening the doors for intentional technology acquisition that could get us there faster. Sounds fancy, but this was hard work with seven days left! This was way more than a slide deck you see in class, or as you would think about it while prepping for an upcoming conference game. It is the practice, film, lifting, eating, more film, roster setup, clear playbook with contingency, all in few days! We didn't have weeks!

Our plan consisted of targeted leverage from our pre-existing technologies and markets coupled with new solutions tied to key global macrotrends segueing into new adjacent market verticals. Good way to think about this is a toolbox. We wanted to sharpen our iron without disrupting what was already working. Where we weren't as strong or didn't have the full tools needed, we created a list of tools to buy. We also looked at good additions that could be added to tools that worked well already but could be enhanced further. The idea was creating new revenue (top line) and margin (bottom line) pathways for long-term growth and elevating the bar further than initially imagined. As athletes, you know you are capable of a lot more than you think most of the time. It is not just a physical game but more so a mental strength game. Try teaching this concept to a risk-averse group. It is like a freshman's first day at conditioning, a rude awakening; more on this in "Chapter 11: Higher Highs and Higher Lows: The People and Processes Are Your Equalizer."

The day arrived! It was the day that the team reported on the plan to the enterprise CEO. I was so proud to have my name on that plan with the team. I always knew we would get there, but I did surprise myself on how clear the vision was translated. I guess that is what happens when you are in the room with the A Team. Many of the A Team members are some of my most cherished mentors to this day! Although I was excited for the day, I was not able to attend the meeting. I was already working on the next growth project for the business I was supporting in Europe! To a layperson, I missed one of the most important professional meetings, but to me, I don't need the trophy. I am on to the REPEAT WIN.

As career athletes, we cherish the championship game win, but we quickly transition to how we can repeat it. We don't do flukes; we like consistency and steady excellence. We become obsessed with winning. That was where my headspace was that day. Within five weeks, I went from feeling like I was drinking from the fire hydrant to being a more poised future executive of a Fortune 100 company. I was no longer just a "best bet." I had officially entered the conversation when talking about the succession pipeline, aka the future Hall of Fame in a Fortune 100 company: One mistake away from not being there, but every chance to be the trailblazer!

When you genuinely believe you are more capable of the next level, you will start to celebrate the roses while you can, but just know, yesterday's success is today's start. This is a business, and your athlete advantage is your differentiator!

As you will come to understand, as we partner together on your new legacy and championship life routine, the best learnings come from trial and error. I urge you to fail often! Let it hurt your pride and shake your being. Why? Because I can pretty much guarantee it will not happen again if the same circumstances present themselves. You will learn from that and develop experiential learning. **Your athlete advantage is FAILING FAST! Failure should not caution you from trying again but rather make you approach it differently and more quickly.** The gem that complements "failing fast" is not "TOLERATING PROBLEMS." If you need a refresher, reread "Chapter 4: Your Athlete Advantage: Catapulting Zero Years of 'Work Experience.'" Remember you can continually fail over and over if you are not truly addressing the real problem. I call this the hamster wheel or working harder, not smarter.

The $10 Billion Project in 5 Weeks

    I live for these opportunities! Challenge your abilities and come out better than you started. This is about the greater purpose and mission, about elevation and drive toward a more holistic personal and professional trajectory. You alone being successful does not make you a leader, but rather rallying the group's bandwidth to believe, find the root cause, blueprint, and operationalize as if it was all their own doing, does. I call this closing the gap.

    Let's get you hungry for identifying and actioning these opportunities when they arise. Being an athlete is a business, so this is not foreign. You may have seen it in a different package. Keep tapping in!

> *Obstacles don't have to stop you. If you run into a wall, don't turn around and give up. Figure out how to climb it, go through it, or work around it.*
>
> —Michael Jordan

Success Beyond Game Day Playbook Recap:

The $10 Billion Project in 5 Weeks: *Fail Fast to Learn Fast and Slow the Game Down*

1. **Go beyond setting goals on** Day 1. Sign them, and now you have a contract.
   a. Write them down, pin them up to see every day, and SHARE THEM—BE INTENTIONAL.
   b. Trust the process and know "drinking from the fire hydrant" will pass.

2. **Identify the problem. Do not tolerate problems**, aka red flags.
   a. Take the hits for the team early on. Show you are about it and willing to take the heat, learn, and acclimate but show a firm/fair approach.
   b. Listen to hear, not listen to speak. Works wonders, but takes practice.

3. **Peel back the layers** and go below the surface. Ask yourself the six whys.
   a. The next learning comes with a proportional change of higher confidence, "slowing the game down" for quicker wins and lower stress and anxiety.
   b. Stay razor-focused and disciplined to the goals while letting situational leadership provide the opportunities to dig, get below the surface, and build the bridge versus trying to be everything to everyone.

4. **Lay the groundwork and foundation** with optionality and flexibility.
   a. Use brick-by-brick mental mapping to drive best outcomes and levers.
   b. Implement change with the team, not to them (BIG LEARNING).

5. **Flawless operationalization**. Game time!
   a. When you have buy-in and trust, this becomes exciting and drives an accountable ownership mindset.
   b. Create vision: you can guide the team to have full pride and purpose and the "ah ha!" becomes their idea and less something you did to get them there! CHECKMATE!

9

Championship Routine in Place

How You Do Anything Is How You Do Everything

The hardest skill to acquire in this sport is the one where you compete all out, give it all you have, and you are still getting beat no matter what you do. When you have the killer instinct to fight through that, it is very special.

—Eddie Reese

In the face of continued success, how do you feel? Do you feel pressure to continue to up the ante? What about in the face of adversity and excitement? Are you the same emotionally? Or do you have a fuse? Do not tell me you do not have emotions. You do have them, but you may be more of a master "suppressor" and/or "compartmentalizer." The fact is, everyone has feelings and a sensory makeup (visual, emotional, auditory, taste, smell, touch) that impacts you in different ways. Think about having an opportunity to publicly speak in front of a sold-out arena of 40,000 fans. You may get an immediate reaction of fear, sweaty palms, heart palpitations, and other physical responses such as hives from thinking about it, right? Or you may feel excited and full of adrenaline.

Listen, I do not hold a PhD in human behavior (I do know many stellar ones who do, though), but I do have an uncanny ability to read people, understand their stress points, and build bridges where often, both sides win. The human side of everything is one of the most important yet underrated areas that I have seen in business. Many people and corporations leverage different yet singular aspects of it, but when you pause, reflect, and truly understand someone's why, you start to realize that the "one size fits all" solutions are not as great as you once thought. **When you shift from "Do onto others as you want done to yourself" to more of "Treat others how they want to be treated" (and mean it!), your success rate changes exponentially.** If you genuinely care about people and impacting their lives for the better, there will always be a seat at the table for you. In this chapter, I break down my view, based on my experience in sports, corporate America, and traveling to 40-plus countries by the age of 34. For me, it came down to reaction and response to all situations and scenarios.

Everyone has different motivations, intentions, passions, and experiences, but if you understand someone's reaction and response mechanism (and triggers), you can start to dig into the "why," which leads to more effective emotional and situational leadership. To grow and scale, you will need a team (fact!). You may think you are doing it all by yourself, but to scale, you will need a team. How you understand and navigate the team will determine your pace and upward trajectory. You may think it is about you and your business, but it is all about people. It is about how people like your product, interact with your product and integrate your product into their lives.

Think about your current team and program; who are you without fans coming to games? Without fans, there is no "top line" revenue, and without revenue, there is no "bottom line" net income and cash. Being an athlete is a business, my friend! Understanding the income statements side of the business enables you to see what the brand generates (in a period of time) for the sales of its products or services (top line), minus all of the investments and costs it took to get the product or service to the market, translating to net income/cash (bottom line).

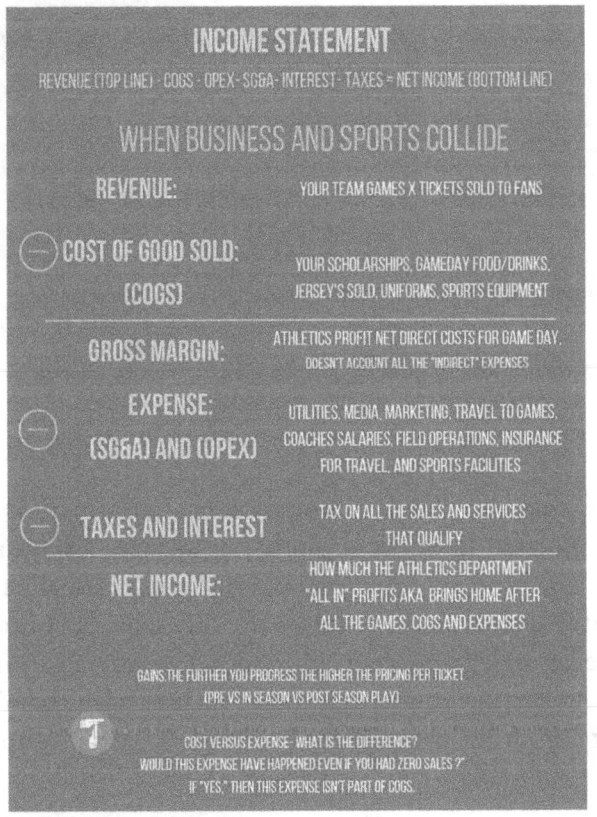

A balance sheet is important, too, as it lays out a company's (in your case, athletic organization's) assets (you and your teammates), liabilities (equipment, running the facilities, paying the staff, utilities, etc.), and ultimately shareholder equity (retained earnings). In simple terms, it helps investors, your fans, to see their return on investment.

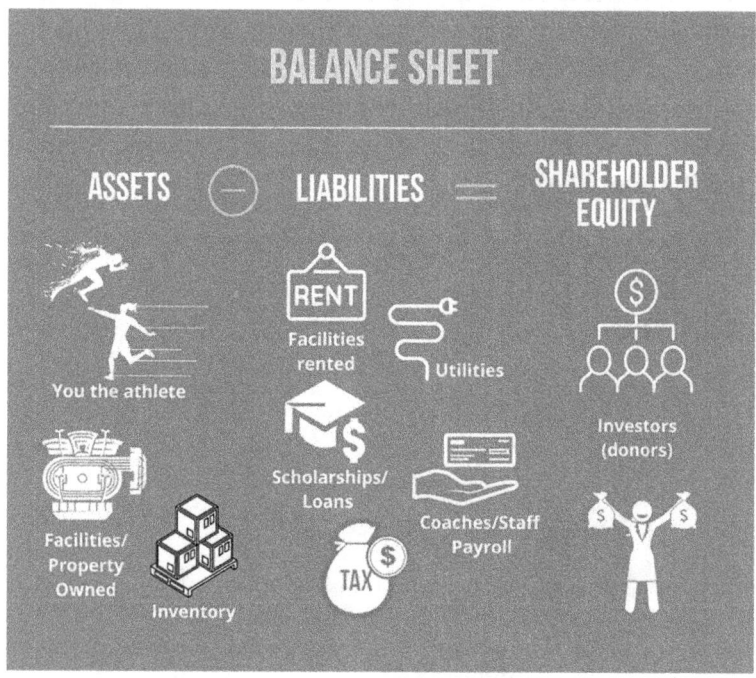

The customer (and your customer's customer) is critically important to know (I didn't say they are always right). Remember, however, you have external and internal customers, and it is paramount to know the difference. For example, your team members are your internal customers, who are critical to driving your speed to the market with the highest quality output for your external customers, the fans. Business

101 is not difficult if you apply the concepts to what you live and breathe daily, straight X's and O's!

If you are young, ambitious, and want to make a name for yourself in your company or team, it is important to learn, early on, what truly drives people's reactions and responses in different circumstances. We all have different triggers that we react and respond to, with some we can easily control and some not so easy to control (straight impulse). **We all have a different "why" that drives us and also makes us unique. Knowing what these are will help you navigate the tempo as you or your team start to "feel all the feels."** Assessing, addressing, and actioning by knowing why people do what they do will translate into consistency and steady results. Situational awareness and poise in chaos are assets in my book! Different incentives drive different behaviors depending on the person.

> Different incentives drive different behaviors depending on the person.

If you want to get into the most important rooms and climb the corporate ladder, then enjoying time off with your friends as an incentive for stellar work won't really interest you as much as being afforded new special projects (like my $10B M&A project) or 1:1 mentorship with a high-up executive. Your reactions and responses to the different opportunities presented will be different. On the contrary, a new expecting mom and dad may cherish time off way more than climbing the ladder, or they may value 50% time off and 50% climbing the ladder. See where I am going? Treating others the way they want to be treated versus how you think they want to be treated are two different things. Not every day is a championship game to people, so be careful with a "one size fits all" approach; be malleable as you grow as a leader.

In each scenario above, there was a different emotional response and energy level for the opportunities presented. In all cases, there is a different part of what I call the "sugar high" emotional lifecycle where you typically operate (the rise once you get the sugar and the body crash after).

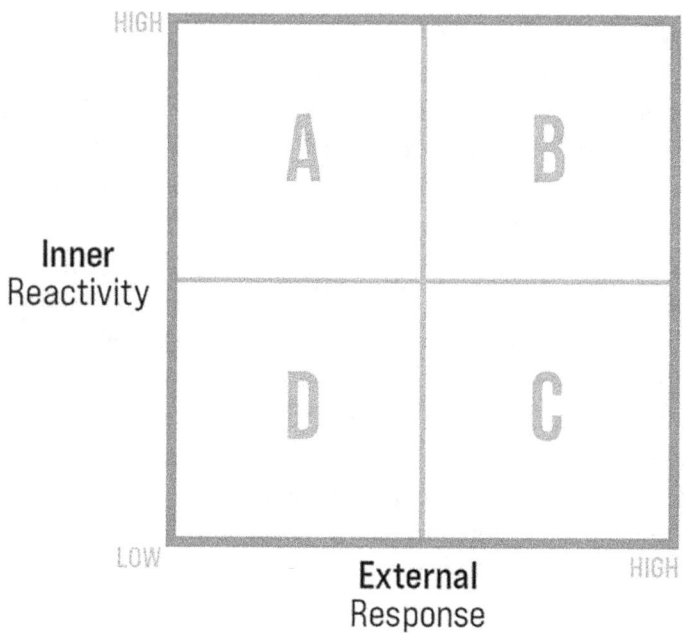

The different quadrants represent different inner reactivity and external response zones. Sometimes you stay in one quadrant while other times you may flex into multiple quadrants. There is no one size fits all! Just like a "sugar high," depending on the person, there is a different climb, length of time you stay in that state, how quickly you come down off your "sugar high" and through the stages how you physically respond.

QUAD MEANINGS:

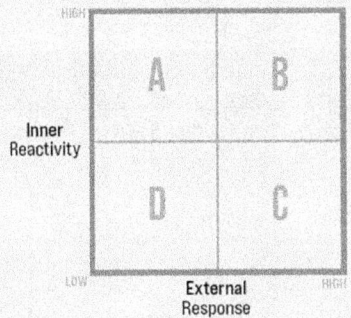

CENTER: Even reactivity and response represent fairly equal parts of being firm but fair, even-keeled and balanced across different scenarios. You flex when needed.

QUAD A: High inner reactivity but low external response means you internally feel all the feels with high intensity, but you either suppress or do not let your emotions get the best of you (show constraint/control over yourself).

QUAD B: High inner reactivity and high external response means you react fast and impulsively respond (bull-in-a-china-shop concept).

QUAD C: Low reactivity but sharp response means you have a short fuse and you respond before you even know what you are reacting to.

QUAD D: Low inner reactivity and low external response means you may be checked out or don't see the value in the moment at hand. You write things off and earmark them as unimportant.

Championship Routine in Place

Below is an example of how I broke myself down professionally and personally. I then compiled how peers and teammates viewed me followed by my coaches and mentors.

SAMMI'S PERSONAL SNAPSHOT

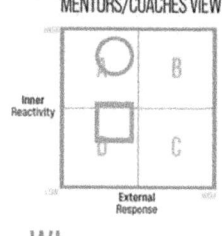

HOW I VIEW MYSELF

Why: Fight between caring for others, listen more than talk, and controlling the controllables. At work, I'm a Type A but personally I am a Type B.

PEERS/OTHERS VIEW

Why: I was always quick to respond, but now I constrain and take the situation one by one instead of all at once.

MENTORS/COACHES VIEW

Why: When warranted, it's good to feel and respond to others to show you care. Moving more to the right quadrant isn't a bad thing.

SAMMI'S PROFESSIONAL SNAPSHOT

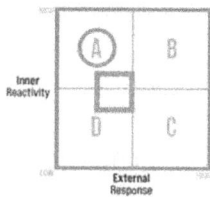 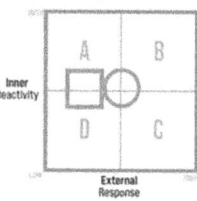 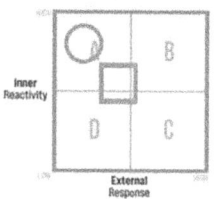

HOW I VIEW MYSELF

Why: Forced into problem solving and course correction within my role. I spend a lot of energy to become authoritative but I really enjoy finding the other future leaders and let them run the show.

PEERS/OTHERS VIEW

Why: I am the one others look to, to get it done. When I flex towards even keeled, not taking point, it throws others off. Working on this.

MENTORS/COACHES VIEW

Why: Fight my urge to want to solve everything because I can get it done faster. I focus on building teams. I have been evolving.

LEGEND: ○ = 80% of the time   ■ = 20% of the time

Take a second and think about where you typically operate, your comfort zone. No right or wrong answer, no judgments, just you, working on better understanding your base state and triggers. Let's use the 80:20 rule with the view of you personally.

1. On the left diagram below, draw and circle *where you think you operate* 80% and draw a square on where you think you operate 20%. Then put a triangle where you want to get to. Under the chart write why you laid out your chart the way you did.

2. In the middle diagram, draw and circle *where you think other teammates think you operate* at 80% and draw a square on where other teammates think you operate 20%. Then put a triangle where you want to get to. Under the chart express why.

3. On the right side, draw and circle *where you think your coaches and mentors think you operate* at 80% and draw a square on where your coaches/mentors think you operate 20%. Then put a triangle where you want to get to. Under the chart express why.

It is OK if you go into multiple quadrants!

Championship Routine in Place

Sugar High Activation

1. On the left diagram (next page), draw and circle where you think you operate 80% and draw a square on where you think you operate 20%. Then put a triangle where you want to get to. Under the chart write why you laid out your chart the way you did.

2. In the middle diagram, draw and circle where you think other teammates think you operate at 80% and draw a square on where other teammates think you operate 20%. Then put a triangle where you want to get to. Under the chart express why.

3. On the right side, draw and circle where you think your coaches and mentors think you operate at 80% and draw a square on where your coaches/mentors think you operate 20%. Then put a triangle where you want to get to. Under the chart express why.

It is OK if you go into multiple quadrants!

HOW I VIEW MYSELF	PEERS/OTHERS VIEW	MENTORS/COACHES VIEW
Inner Reactivity — A / B / D / C — External Response	Inner Reactivity — A / B / D / C — External Response	Inner Reactivity — A / B / D / C — External Response

Why: _____

Why: _____

Why: _____

LEGEND: ⭕ = 80% of the time   ◻ = 20% of the time

I challenge you to have open conversations with teammates and coaches about how you react and respond in different situations. You will learn a lot! Sometimes what we think we know is far from the actual truth. Go to the source and assess. In about one to four weeks, relook at what you put on the charts above and assess if it is still consistent. If not, draw over with another color and write why your position changed. This will be eye-opening. Another way you can acquire the information is a 360 assessment. It will anonymously allow whoever you ask to participate to give an unfiltered, unbiased response of how people view you. I took a 360 every year and tracked my progress and saw if there were patterns. Always a lesson to leverage my curiosity and thirst-quenching.

> Sometimes what we think we know is far from the actual truth. Go to the source and assess.

Sometimes it takes that mundane championship routine every day, no matter what, to show your consistency matches your intention and your drive doesn't come with a blind, big ego. Remember that most, if not all, do not care about your struggle, your journey, or what sacrifices you made to get to the top. Many only come to you once you are at the top and completely disregard what it took to get you there. Just think about that: You build your brand, struggle, and make sacrifices by yourself daily for your future self-stock value while every day being your own cheerleader while no one is watching. This right here is where many athletes either succeed or struggle post-sports. What you must remember is that you have already done this to be able to play at the highest levels! Leverage the learnings derived from no one knowing who you were before college or pro. Peel the onion's layers back.

Just remember to pause when you feel a spiral and find ways to reel yourself in because nine out of 10 times, as an athlete, you have been there, done that. If you know who you are and can be disciplined to put in the work, then you are money! But if you doubt who you are and your self-doubt is navigating you, then you will have to grow through what you go through. The mental part of navigating post-sports was one of the hardest aspects I had to go through. But just like me, you will get through it!

The journey, your mental headspace, and your determination to be successful in life is where the magic lies and most likely where your heartstrings lie! Many will throw all the reverse psychology at you, like "Give me a chance; I am the underdog" or "Don't get too big for the little people" or "All I am asking for is five minutes." I am here to remind you to close the gap and operate with others at your level or further up. Raise the bar! Who you hang out with and conduct business with is who you are. You are on an onward and upward trajectory. As a famous rapper said, "Yesterday's price is not today's price." Don't cheapen your stock value. From the activation above, we are further sharpening your iron and elevating your toolbox. **Knowledge is power, and digging beyond surface level takes practice.**

When you find the person who asks, "How did you overcome when faced with adversity, challenges after challenges, walls crashing in, and when you felt like giving up but somehow pushed through?" or "What information helped you acquire the best knowledge that provided a step change for you?" this is the person (or people) with whom you take the meeting. Your approach and curiosity to learn is what will differentiate you. People will test you, see how far they can take you, and push your pressure points, so let's work them out now in our safe space.

How you react and respond through all situations is an important craft to master in business and life. Even though you may not want to, you can be an introvert and still speak flawlessly and be well poised in front of large crowds. On the contrary, you can be an extrovert, full of energy, like to be the center of attention, yet fumble over the opportunity, even though you felt it was well within your wheelhouse. Over the next few chapters, we are going to granularly work through your responses, actions, and leveraging abilities when faced with a blank sheet of paper in front of you. Just know, you are equipped with all you need, and all you and I are going to do is peel the onion's layers back. You are an athlete; you are built for this!

Using the activation exercise above as a guide, would you say you are levelheaded throughout your ups and downs journey thus far, or does the current moment seem to get to you? Be honest with yourself. There is no right or wrong answer here. This is an important aspect in helping build who you are today and harnessing it as a leveraging building block for the future. Do not shortchange yourself here; think! Be intentional! The reason why this is so important (just as important as your goals) is **many people give up what they want most in the future for what they want today.** All emotion. Let that sink in! You will need to focus on pushing away shortsightedness for foresight. It is difficult, especially if you are impatient like me! Success in life and wealth generation is all about understanding people (and emotions), establishing structure, education, discipline, and patience!

> Success in life and wealth generation is all about understanding people (and emotions), establishing structure, education, discipline, and patience!

It took a lot of energy and dedicated work to get to a productive use of foresight. It is normal to feel overwhelmed through the process. I would lose sleep over challenging my speed to problem-solve and ability to course-correct fast enough. I was so fixed on fixing things that I wasn't looking at what was working well first! Let me add, this affected every aspect of my life, including relationships (need I say more?). I had to break out of a habit that I had spent my whole life creating. You will, too. I had to challenge my mental game to think bigger, even though everything in me was saying to go back to my "muscle memory" base state. **Elevation requires separation! That is tried and true, trust me! Do not downplay getting your mental side in check, relationship baggage discharged, and overall health in order because these three components are a requirement for success and wealth generation.** There are levels to this game, and mastering the emotional aspects while also staying disciplined to your contract is what will get you into any room at any time, period.

No matter the learning and coaching, I have always found a way to utilize momentum. Just like you do when a major turn of events during a game occurs. From the piercing chants, screams, and stadium rumble to the wave of emotional responses from the crowd after a goal, point, touchdown, or home run is undeniable. It turns it from a game for entertainment to more of a way of life for fans. I always think about soccer (or futbol, as most of the world says it) and the highly charged emotion in the game, from the acting skills of the players on the field to the fans belching out screams and chants as if their livelihoods were at stake and the outcome or change in pace of the game was on their shoulders. If you do not believe me, go to Europe and get a feel for how they play. Some good matches are the Derby D'Italia (Inter Milan and Juventus), North London Derby (Arsenal and Tottenham), Madrid Derby (Real Madrid and Athlético Madrid), and even the Intercontinental Derby (Galatasaray and Fenerbahce). It is about prestige and honor, with passion driving the boat.

Or think of an MMA fight where it is borderline *Fight Club* mixed with fans yelling like a bunch of unsatiable savages. Your impact on the field can change someone's mood—straight powerful. Do you now see the importance of understanding human behavior and the emotional side of things? Human behavior and emotional strings, if utilized and harnessed correctly, can work melodiously for you personally and professionally. With knowledge and practice, you can change how you react, change outcomes, and change your impact on others. You should never doubt your ability to run your own business or venture because you have been navigating the ups and downs for years through sports.

As athletes, we are intense! We compete every day and even over the smallest things. We have that inner beast mode where excuses are not an option, ever! But there are also many layers to all of us, most unexplored. We put our personal feelings to the side for the betterment of the team. It is a delicate balance to break the muscle memory here. It is important to keep a team-focused, open-minded approach but also important for you to explore *you* and how you handle things without the backing of a team. I got lost a few times post-sports and would overcompensate by obsessing over being results-oriented, going above and beyond, challenging, and competing to win every day in every interaction, even though I was tired and didn't feel like I was being myself. I never took a pulse check.

I had this corporate avatar that had garnered the attention in all the major rooms, and I had expectations to live up to! I craved belonging in every interaction, with every person, and in every group, in this massive $40B company—not practical, right? This was my normal mantra at the time. I didn't say it was healthy. How I moved (warp speed), never taking a pause

Championship Routine in Place

for a breath of fresh air, started to impact me personally by not allowing me to keep my emotions in check. I became a master compartmentalizer, but for what?

In corporate America, I was giving everything I had but personally had nothing to give. It was hard for people to approach me, even though they thought the world of me. I was moving at warp speed, literally. At the same time, I let my emotions determine how I traded in the stock market (BIG NO-NO; more on this in Chapter 10), while obsessively wanting to climb the corporate ladder faster. I was breaking my No. 1 rule: Do not make decisions when you are mad, angry, or happy. Always be even-keeled. I never checked in and "felt all the feels" because I was hyper-focused.

Sometimes it takes a rude awakening to force the change. I took a weekend vacation to Europe, by myself, and couldn't unwind, had anxiety (never had this before), and got majorly sick. The act of "slowing down" and taking R&R started to shock my highly charged system physically and mentally. PAUSE! This right here is an example of a major bad! What I needed to do all along was ask for help! I needed to work smarter, not harder! Remember, the higher you go, the thinner the air, the lonelier it gets, but it doesn't mean you do not ask for help! This was my first taste of surface-level top success. Do you know the feeling? Do you give everything you have on the field so that you have no more left off the field? Do you just shut the social side down most of the time? Are you afraid it will distract you from your purpose and mission?

I quickly realized that I needed to leverage my resources and momentum and ask for formal mentorship. I asked for structured corporate resources that targeted managing my bull-in-a-china-shop emotions, made response/ambition tradeoffs, and developed my situational leadership and emotional intelligence. You will never get what you don't ask for, so ask! I had champions, supporters, and my ambition, so I received full access, thankfully. You cannot be effective for your business or sports career if you are not personally good with yourself, long-term! You may be able to survive short-term setbacks, but long-term, nope! Let me go on the record and say, **EVERYONE NEEDS COACHING!**

Think about it this way; I was using my "even reactivity and response sugar high" to climb the corporate ladder and the "low reactivity and low response sugar crash" for my social life, my personal health, and inconsistent relationships. I didn't know any differently! As athletes, sacrifice is a way of life, and we deal with the cards given, no excuses! Oh, how much I have learned since 2014! The version of me today smirks at who I was in 2014, but, hey, **"Grow through what you go through" is a mantra of mine!**

> **As athletes, sacrifice is a way of life, and we deal with the cards given, no excuses!**

Whether you were recruited or a walk-on, there were "best bets" put on your future performance at all levels within your athletic organization. Fact! There may be different levels of pressure put on you versus others, but everyone has a Day 1. **Every move and interaction you make from Day 1 forward drives your stock value. The pressure and intensity never go away. It just gets magnified. How you handle and respond to the pressure is where your BIG promotions come!** For you, if you make a "Top 10 *SportsCenter*" in OT during the national championship when the pressure is on for the "W," I promise there will be positive outfall in some capacity! It could be a confirmed starting spot next season, brands wanting to pay for your likeness or more limelight, and media attention (if this interests you). Same applies in corporate America. Do you get where I am going with this? You have already learned or are currently building your resume by being a high-performing athlete. A program will not just add anyone to the team; the stakes are too high, and guess what? They picked you!

I know you can handle the heat of being an athlete when the opportunities present themselves, but can you handle the pressure of guaranteeing results beyond your comfort zone that are wildly foreign to you? The higher you go, the less room for error, and the more complex and visible you get to some of the biggest decision makers and rooms. How you handle and respond to the responsibility and pressure bestowed upon you is what makes or breaks you as a leader. You may not have signed up for the pace, politics, and/or pressure, but it is in your lap to take care of, so what do you do about that? Deal with it like a champ! Yet another parallel from sports to corporate America.

Like I said, **being an athlete is a business**, and you are an employee working toward your big promotion at this point. Pressure and stress will always be there, front and center. Are you diversifying your talent and resources to mitigate risk, or are you full speed ahead, the sky's the limit? Do you have a plan B and C, if needed (this one is IMPORTANT)?

As we embark on more lucrative changes for you to learn as you grow your personal and professional stock worth, just know we are going to open your view to different financial structures and pathways to grow as you grow. We are now entering shark-infested waters. At this point, you should (or need to) know who you are and where you want to go, have a contract in place, have willingness to dive straight in and be able to emotionally check yourself because the remaining part of this book is highly charged and full of activation. Don't believe me?

Next up: In all things, notch it up!

- Continuing to check your emotional reactions and responses
- Negotiating globally with different cultural biases
- The living now or saving to spend later tradeoff, with money at stake
- Stock Market 101 and your readiness (fail fast)
- Real Estate 101
- Crypto gains
- Leveraging assets without touching them
- Cash versus cash flow

This game isn't for everyone, but I have this feeling you are ready for the challenge. Bet!

Success Beyond Game Day Playbook Recap:

Championship Routine in Place: *How You Do Anything Is How You Do Everything*

Here are my learnings on emotional intelligence and situational leadership. Take a second to apply these concepts to your day-to-day.

1. Understanding what is truly important to someone and how they prioritize different things in different ways is key. Pay attention to how others want to be treated, not how you think they want to be treated. Spend the time and learn what makes people tick. It pays dividends!

2. You can be the best at what you do, and others may respect you, but if they are afraid to approach you, you lose assets and gain more liabilities. Don't let blind ambition drive the boat. Be mindful and inclusive for diversity of thought.

3. Keeping the pedal down to elevate and not getting comfortable is important, but don't think you need to be so obsessed that you feel guilt for having a social life.

4. Not striving for perfection can lead to more holistic, positive, long-term outcomes with financial gains instead of getting yourself and the team bogged down in details that you won't get paid for or won't increase your stock value.

5. Genuinely approaching business with a bridge-building mentality and establishing your gut on being a good judge of characters will be key. Business relationships are an extension of you and your brand.

6. Embrace each day with curiosity and open-mindedness because change will come. Identifying and adapting to change will help you navigate yourself and others.

7. Steer away from negative self-talk, but when it comes (because it will), being able to recognize, pause, reframe, and restart will be important. Great area to ask for help to guide you through in a more structured way. I did!

8. Listen to hear, not listen to talk (I actively work on this).

9. How you do anything is how you do everything. Be mindful that there are many people who may be watching and waiting for your reaction, so lead with intention and confidence, but always be people-forward! You will have to make tough decisions, but never do that at the expense of people's well-being.

10. Sometimes being a bull in a china shop just doesn't do it; sometimes you can catch more flies with honey than with vinegar. Being polite and empathetic can open doors that being rude could never. (This is where I got coached up—big time!)

10

Being an Athlete Is a Business

Use Your Winning Building Blocks Beyond Game Day for Lucrative Outcomes

Champions keep playing until they get it right.

—Billie Jean King

As the profound and mega-powerhouse Denzel Washington once said, "Without commitment, you'll never start, but more importantly, without consistency, you'll never finish.... Keep working, keep striving, never give up, fall down seven times, get up eight. Ease is a greater threat to progress than hardship."

What happens when the lights go out and you may not be playing anymore? After thinking through what (and why) is important in your life, are you ready to tell me who you are beyond sports? Will you commit to sharpening your innate and acquired skills with an *established structure* to carry you to your next championship game, your legacy, and annuity success? I believe in you to make that choice.

I emphasize structure because as you build your championship routine, establishing your financial wealth structure is part of your overall winning strategy. It can serve as your backup and can free you from feeling trapped in a job to finding a passion you can monetize. Money may not be the end-all, be-all, but it provides the means to do the things that are needed in this world. **Your ability to spring into action, lead with intention, drive with knowledge, embody patience, continuously improve your emotional maturity, and build your legacy structure is where we are headed.** Easy peasy, right?

Think about some of the biggest athletes or entertainers who are known for their stellar investments. What about the ones who have had multimillions but went broke? As reported by *Sports Illustrated* in March 2009, other athletes from the nation's 3 biggest and most profitable leagues—the NBA, NFL, and Major League Baseball—are suffering from a financial pandemic. By the time they have been retired for two years, 78% of former NFL players have gone bankrupt or are under financial stress because of joblessness or divorce. Within 5 years of retirement, an estimated 60% of former NBA players are broke. "Athletes have a different set of challenges from, say, entertainers," says money manager Michael Seymour, the founder of Philadelphia-based UNI Private Wealth Strategies. "There's a far shorter peak earnings period [in sports] than in any other profession, and in many cases, they lack the time and desire to understand and monitor their investments."

It happens to a lot of people! And listen, I know many great financial advisors out there, but I also know a lot who prey on the "uninformed." Just because you have an advisor doesn't mean you will grow your money. Wise up, whippersnapper; this is the level-up season where you can have a business team around you, but you always need to be on your game, be able to take a pulse and assert checks and balances. **If people know you know something, they will be less**

Being an Athlete Is a Business

inclined to pull a short one by you, unless they just don't care (which is possible).

It is Human Behavior 101 that when an easy opportunity and a more challenging one present themselves, people are more drawn to the easy side of things. It takes less energy! As athletes, you may aim to leverage the easier route, but you do not fear challenge, so you are already ahead of the majority! Imagine you making millions and have no clue on the structure or how anything works. Do you think it will be tempting for others who are advising or around you to try to over-leverage you, especially if you have no clue?! We see all the time about different stars and players declaring bankruptcy or going to court for unpaid rent for their mega-mansion. Have you ever seen coverage on how their advisor or agent is living during the thick of an athlete's trials and tribulations? I am pretty sure they have a hedge in place and are living their best life. Irking, isn't it? The growth comes from how you rebound after the setback and reshape your reactivity versus response. I am hopeful we will help you avoid these circumstances.

> **It is Human Behavior 101 that when an easy opportunity and a more challenging one present themselves, people are more drawn to the easy side of things. It takes less energy!**

Roger Staubach, a Heisman Trophy winner, US Navy man, and Super Bowl MVP as the Dallas Cowboys quarterback, was one of the first athletes to play professional sports and work as a real estate broker in the offseason. He found a way to expand his real estate portfolio across the US, and his business was acquired by Jones Lang LaSalle for +$600M in 2008. Michael Jordan made billions, more than he ever did playing ball, off his Air Jordan sneaker brand, endorsement deals (Hanes, Gatorade, etc.), and investments in the Hornets and Sportrader. According to Forbes, he invested ~$175M in the majority purchase of the Charlotte Hornets in 2010, and it **took nine to 10 years to turn that into ~$1.3B**. Kobe Bryant co-funded Bryant Stibel, an investment firm that led to investments in Dell, Fortnite, and Alibaba. Kobe personally invested $6M in BodyArmor (sports drink) in 2014, which **seven years later resulted** in his estate making $400M (now worth +$700M) from Coca-Cola acquiring BodyArmor.

The woman powerhouse Serena Williams leveraged her endorsements and founded Serena Ventures, concentrated on helping minority and women businesses with a focus on food, fashion, health, and ecommerce. Some of her notable companies and investments are her company S By Serena, her position as a board member of Poshmark and SurveyMonkey, and her investment in the Kopi Kenengan coffee line (along with many more). Maria Sharapova has a marketing empire with Nike and Porsche, launched a candy business, Sugarpova, and invested in the wellness brand Therabody.

And then there is Shaq! This man is invested in car washes, gyms, the Ring doorbell (same as Nas), was an early Google and Apple investor, owns restaurants like Krispy Kreme, Papa John's, Auntie Annie's, and Five Guys. I am confident he is also big into the real estate game, too, just like Alex Rodriguez is with his investment firm, Monument Capital Management. A-Rod founded A-Rod Corp, which he utilized for investments in Snapchat, VitaCoco, and NRG eSports.

One of my favorite rappers, Nas, is quite the ingenious man. If you only think about Nas as a rapper, then educate yourself. He has made many investments, such as in Dropbox and Casper Sleep, but his big changemaker, in my opinion, was Ring and Coinbase. He had the foresight and developed Queensbridge Venture Partners in 2013, which became an early investor in Coinbase (cryptocurrency exchange). **According to Forbes, Nas took a ~$100-$500K investment** in 2013 and flipped it to +$40-$200M during the Coinbase IPO in 2021, about eight years later!

Do you see what I am illustrating? **This is generational wealth, ladies and gentlemen! There is not quick turnkey solution, and it takes time and patience.** If anyone is selling that, run! To generate wealth, you need to diversify your portfolio and work smarter, not harder! Having the right headspace, being willing to reprogram against your comfort and familiarity, and aligning with the right network can pretty much set you up for your net worth to grow and get you a major seat at the table.

> Having the right headspace, being willing to reprogram against your comfort and familiarity, and aligning with the right network can pretty much set you up for your net worth to grow and get you a major seat at the table.

A portfolio means a collection of investments. But a lucrative, well-positioned portfolio means a collection of high-value assets both short- and long-term. This is where I want to arm you with knowledge to make the best decision for you! Learn from my learnings and try some new things! Thus far, we have translated your personal and professional value as "stock value" with you being an appreciating asset, going up in value year after year. It is like going from your high school star rating to your draft king odds bets in Vegas to your stock value being translated into a video game! There is so much out there to grab if you open your eyes, align, and apply yourself. **As an appreciating asset, you gain access to other assets and grow your net worth. This right here is how the wealthy get wealthier; do not sleep on this!**

Think about your team. If you have a championship organization that invests in the right caliber players, like yourself, and promotes runways for growth (on and off the field), don't you think other highly sought-out players will want to come play with you and your team in the future? **Younger athletes want to feel what you feel and be their own unique version of what you are while envisioning leaving their own mark. Shoot, if you are aspiring to play pro, there will be others you look up to and work to break their records as well.** Understanding how someone moves and their reactivity versus response as well as granularly knowing what is important to them and how to connect, will be key in the wealth game! Being an athlete and role model is a big responsibility, so why not be well rounded on and off the field? You have been making important and extremely pivotal choices your whole life and sports career.

Some of the INTENTIONAL choices many athletes make through their athletic journey:

- Assessing who you need to align with or avoid (I can count on one hand)
- Finding the right coach and team for year-round play (I would fly out of state for travel ball)
- Practicing or staying low-key when your friends are having a night out (daily sacrifice)
- Having a job to pay for your gear and help the family out the best way you can
- Picking the college program you will attend that will mold you further (oh, the process/pressure! I will leave this one for a rainy day)
- Training with the best off-season crew to get you pro ready (tens of thousands of dollars in investment)
- If you get injured, flipping the mental beast mode switch for the "comeback," where no one can find you, but they all know you are working, versus letting your injury define

Being an Athlete Is a Business

your outcome (this one right here was big for me when I had my neck injury)

Apply your approach and beast mode to new concepts and opportunities so you can impact generations to come. That's when you know you made it! Let's start with thinking about the word *currency*.

As defined by Merriam-Webster Dictionary, *currency* is a medium of exchange (an instrument or system to facilitate a sale) or circulation for goods and services with a standard value. Your mastery of currency and how to generate wealth in forms of the stock market (long-term stocks, options, 401K, Roth IRA, traditional IRA), real estate (land, house, apartment building, parking lot), Airbnb/Vrbo cash flow model, and/or other passive income streams gives you access to and many times can solidify your seat at the table. There are levels to this game! I am throwing a lot at you, so let's focus on the basics, for now. Don't worry: When I come to collaborate with you and your team, we will drill down on all aspects! This is all about you and the information you need to succeed. You are the reason I am here!

You may often hear, "It takes money to make money," right? What happens if you do not have money to even start? Glad you asked—thank you. There is no too-small amount of money to start with; building starts with one brick at a time. It may take sacrifice, but anything is possible when you want it bad enough. Prioritize! Let's dig into those Nikes you may have on (not issued, but you bought). Let's play out the game of to buy or not to buy for the Off-White x Nike Air Force 1 Low "Volt" collection. Or think about that one thing that hits your soft spot that you splurge on. You may even feel an emotional connection because to you, they are more than just the material items. The design and intricate details are well thought out, down to the granular layer, and you appreciate those little subtle "iykyk" details. I am confident that you like when others react when you flash them, too (I will leave this one here). If you are like me, anything unique, rare, "one of ones" that are hard to access by the masses is my speed. I get it!

Some might even say these Off-White x Nike Air Force 1 Low Volts are an investment, while others say they are just a sneaker. If you lead with saying, these can resale at a value of greater than 300%, then I may entertain your proof point to add this as part of your portfolio. I am all about thoughtful debate! Be honest: Can you actually wear the shoes and keep them in mint condition? Where is the fun in saying you own them? If you are already willing to not crease or wear them more than a few times to keep them in mint condition, then why not invest in Nike stock with the $700 to $1,000 you intended to spend on the shoes and sit until the share price goes up? Would you be interested in being disciplined and patient to take one asset and make two assets?

The S&P 500 stock market return since 1991 has averaged 8% (with inflation) to 10% (non-inflation adjusted). The S&P 500 stands for The Standard and Poor's 500, which tracks the top 500 companies listed on the stock exchanges in the United States. Some examples of the different exchanges are the New York Stock Exchange (NYSE) and the NASDAQ. Within that average, you may have some companies grow faster than the S&P, at 10-30% per year, depending on the company fundamentals (buzz and relevant things going on). Look at Nike's performance since 2015. Does this look like a good stock to you to invest in? What do you see?

Being an Athlete Is a Business

A good rule of thumb that I have learned from the best in the game is if you can't buy something you want at least 3x that amount, then you walk away. You are not ready. Remember what we just went over last chapter: **Manage your reactivity and response, and throw your ego out of the picture. It is not a forever thing; it is just an "until you get it" thing.** Some say at least 2x the amount, but for me, I am all about 3x.

> **A good rule of thumb that I have learned from the best in the game is if you can't buy something you want at least 3x that amount, then you walk away. You are not ready.**

The latest estimated Off-White x Nike Air Force 1 Volts retailed for an average of $850. By my rule of thumb that translates into adding $2,550 (3x $850) to your brokerage account. Think of a brokerage account where you can hold, buy, or sell investments like stocks. You need an account to trade in the game. For example, let's say you bought on January 27, 2021, a total of 19 shares at a total starting investment of $2,489.38. What would $2,489.38 in Nike shares get you within 2021?

Look at the daily 2021 Nike chart below. Your initial investment was $2,489.38 and in nine days, February 9, 2021, was now worth $2,757.09, an unrealized profit of $267.71! Think of unrealized profit as money that you have tied into a stock position based on a positive move up, but you haven't sold it just yet. When you cash out your profits, then you realize them! This means you would have an asset delivering value and continuing to grow while inching toward 31% of the total cost of the Off-White x Nike Air Force 1 Volt. You just turned one asset (depending on if you are reselling them) into two! Not to mention, as an athlete, when you wear Nike, you give them free advertisement (unless sponsored), so why not leverage and turn your brand promotion into more unrealized Nike gains because you are a shareholder?! I told you there are levels to this game! By August 5, 2021, in less than a year, you would have been able buy your sneakers! **The power of information and structure can set you free. You will start learning that you have the means to get what you want while growing your money!**

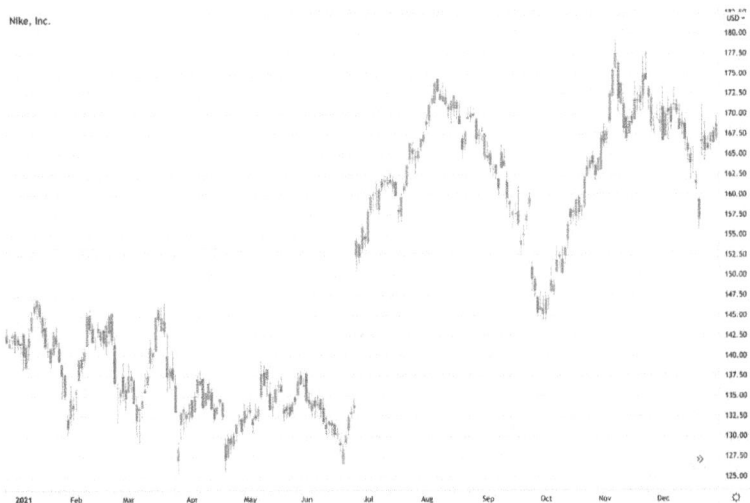

Financial Definition Net Profit = Revenue - Expense

Definition applied Nike Example Money for your Sneakers= Point in time stock price x 19 shares owned - initial $2489.38 investment

Being an Athlete Is a Business

Starting Funds	$2,489.38				
Purchased on Jan 27 2021	$ 131.02	per share			
Total Shares Owned	19	shares			
	5-Feb	5-May	5-Aug	5-Nov	6-Dec
Per share Price	$ 145.11	$ 132.21	$ 173.85	$ 177.51	$ 168.91
Total Shares Value	$2,757.09	$ 2,511.99	$ 3,303.15	$ 3,372.69	$ 3,209.29
Net Total Profit	$ 267.71	$ 22.61	$ 813.77	$ 883.31	$ 719.91
% profit gain vs shoe price	31%	3%	96%	104%	85%
Takeaway: Patience! Wealth takes TIME and PATIENCE!					

The market will go up and down, but it moves onward and upward with higher highs and higher lows, outside of great depressions. I am not making this up; the below is a real S&P 500 chart over the last 15 years based off real trades in the US stock market. Think of the S&P 500 (Standard and Poor's 500) as a representation, aka index, of the performance for the top 500 companies in the USA.

This right here is breaking your fixed view and naïve understanding of value, assets, and how you should spend your money. I apply this concept to every aspect of my life.

Any Starbucks coffee I get, I put 3x the amount of a latte in my brokerage, own the stock, and the gains pay for my coffee for free—go figure! You can shift from aimless into targeted and mindful. **I am helping you understand it isn't just about saving as much as understanding where you are placing your money for more leverage. I am still on the journey; it will never end!** That is the fun part! The pursuit of greatness and generational wealth is so important to me, I have spent +$50K in coaching and programs to get me the right tools. All I have done since then is set up the structure and let my money work for itself.

As a highly successful mogul and multi-millionaire once said to me, "The first million is hard, but the second is inevitable.… It's not becoming a millionaire that's important. It's the person you must become in order to become a millionaire. You have to become a completely different person. You have to develop character beyond 99% of the people in the world. You have to develop honesty and discipline and quality relationships and the willingness and the ability to work and set priorities…because without that, nothing is possible."

If (and WHEN) you establish this mentality, imagine your power scaling 10x. I have laid out the literal meaning based on the recent Nike example. Instead of investing $2,489.30 in Nike shares, let's say you invest 10x the amount, at $24,893. How does it play out in 2022 for you? Well, you get 10x more gains! Once you start to establish yourself and gain a scaling advantage, it will help you grow even faster. It is equivalent to sitting at the millionaire blackjack table compared to the thousands blackjack table. You may have the same skills, but you sit at the table where you are able to compete today. You stay focused on work every day to get to the next table. Then when you are at the millionaire table, that may not be enough. Success and progress is addicting! Do not get lost and try to play above your means; brick by brick, investment by investment, you will set yourself up for success.

Same example with Nike, but instead of $2,489.30, you put in $24,893.80 (10x):

			5-Feb	5-May	5-Aug	5-Nov	6-Dec
Starting Funds	$ 24,893.80						
Purchased on Jan 27 2021	$ 131.02	per share					
Total Shares Owned	190	shares					
Per share Price		$	145.11	$ 132.21	$ 173.85	$ 177.51	$ 168.91
Total Shares Value		$	27,570.90	$ 25,119.90	$ 33,031.50	$ 33,726.90	$ 32,092.90
Net Total Profit		$	2,677.10	$ 226.10	$ 8,137.70	$ 8,833.10	$ 7,199.10
% profit gain vs shoe price			315%	27%	957%	1039%	847%
Takeaway: Scale is a gamechanger! You make 10x the total net profit! Oh, what one decimal to the right can do for your life!							

You make 10x the total net profit! Oh, what one decimal to the right can do for your life!

Based upon the basics thus far, why would you keep your money in a banking savings account only earning 0.1% to 3% (maybe 6% if it's a high-yielding account) when you can grow your money by 10% each year in the stock market? If you had $200,000 in a bank and you wanted to withdraw it all today, the bank may say they don't have that much cash on site to give to you or question if you are in trouble. They may need to "call their manager." Why is that? The fact is, they take your money that they hold for you and guarantee 0.1%-3% yield on your base money annually, while they offer other people loans at higher interest rates or even put the money into the stock market index funds. So, they can make 8-10% off your money that you are saving (as a nest egg or for rainy day), and while they "hold and borrow" your capital money, you only get 0.1%-3%. Does that seem right or make sense to you? Why not let your money make you money while you borrow against your asset to fund the acquisition of new assets like real estate?

Oh, how the real estate cash flow and borrowing against your assets (LOC and LMA) can change your scale advantage! This right here is where I am currently and actively working to get smarter. I am growing through what I am going through, and it is so exciting! I have the absolute privilege of learning from Grant Cardone's 10X real estate university (I will leave the details for our F2F!). Such great coaching, diversity of thought, strategies, and learnings! I told you, everyone needs a coach in different aspects of your life! Then what you acquire and implement that you can pass down to others! Now do you understand why I am here? I am here for you!

One of the major benefits of owning land or real estate is it can serve as a hedge to inflation. Think about it; there is only so much land in the world, right? If you have a finite amount of supply, the population growing, and demand increasing, that directly translates into the prices going up (aka appreciation)! I'll repeat the famous rapper's infamous quote again: "Yesterday's price is not today's price." When you have an asset that appreciates and doesn't lose its inherent value, in the financial world, they call this intrinsic value (we discussed this briefly earlier). Think about areas where back in the day, they were completely different from what they are today, booming. Ownership and equity are everything!

Ownership and equity are everything!

Real estate also has many tax benefits! Levels to this! Just know you can buy an asset (such as a home) and swap to buy a bigger property by means of a 1031 to defer your capital gains and build wealth. The tax game will be addressed during our face-to-face, and I will come with a seasoned pro next

Being an Athlete Is a Business

to me. I never said I was an expert in all things, but I did mention that I know a good bit; and even more importantly, I know a lot of smart, elite people who add tons of value to the wealth game!

I lived in Hoboken (home of Frank Sinatra), New Jersey, for eight years, and the views I saw were shocking in the early days. Hoboken sits right outside of the Holland Tunnel going into Manhattan, New York, so you can say it has one of the best, if not the best, view of the NYC skyline. The land value and popularity of Hoboken has increased by more than 100x, a major transfer of wealth for those who invested in the '60s and '70s. Remember, it takes foresight, discipline, and patience. This value took a couple decades to achieve. *The key is to avoid giving up what you want in the future for what you want today.*

The world and financial landscape are ever changing! Think about when Uber and Lyft came into the shared and personal car service industry. Initially, many thought the concept couldn't work because you would be riding in strangers' cars. But look at Uber and Lyft today; they completely decentralized the taxi system. Some countries are fighting it, but eventually it will be a universally accepted business model. Now you have many taxi drivers also utilizing the app platforms. Another relevant example is Airbnb and Vrbo and their impact on the hospitality industry. Initially, the market reacted by thinking: Why would anyone want to stay in a stranger's home, not in their own sheets? But look at the landscape today. Globally, you can get access to most unique places and experiences with the comfort of home amenities that are important to you. Some of the big hoteliers have had to improvise and adapt.

Same theoretical concept for cryptocurrency. Crypto is decentralizing the banking system. The interesting concept here is it delineates against inflation and maintains its inherent intrinsic value. The government can print money and increase inflation, and your investment still holds its value. It does come with cons as well, given it is still early in the overall global adoption, but it sure is picking up pace. Educate yourself or get left behind! According to the Binance Academy[4], blockchains are secured through a variety of mechanisms that include advanced cryptographic techniques and mathematical models of behavior and decision making. Think game theory on steroids! Blockchain technology is the underlying structure of most cryptocurrency systems and is what prevents this kind of digital money from being duplicated or destroyed.

On the meta universe side of things, Binance Academy shares with you that it is conceptually a future iteration of the internet that will enable you to work, meet, game, and socialize together in its 3D spaces. I know, it seems far out there, just like NFTs (non-fungible tokens). NFTs are uniquely marked virtual assets that could represent real assets and are protected under the blockchain. There is a lot of debate about crypto, the meta universe, and NFTs, so arming yourself with information and your curiosity could potentially lead to some great investment breakthroughs. Only you can determine where you take your best bets. I will leave you with

Being an Athlete Is a Business

this fundamental question: Do you want to be like Kodak, which went from innovating for centuries to bankruptcy in 2012 based on bad decisions and an inability to adapt with the changing market needs? You will need to adapt and be nimble, as the world and financial landscape is changing!

I went many years trying to learn this all by myself while trying to grow my "stock worth." I was working harder, not smarter, although I was profitable (not as profitable as I could have been). Remember what I mentioned in the last chapter: Everyone needs a coach and mentorship! It all changed for me from 2019 to 2021 when I started interfacing and being coached by the real-deal elite levelers. Those coaches started with $3-$10K and flipped it to +$30-$50M by establishing structure, studying, and putting emotional checks in place (shout-out to Tay Sweat!). I knew a lot about the mechanics, but Tay taught me the right entrance and exit approach like a melodious symphony. He helped me to tap into what I knew already: discipline, patience, constant studying, and managing reactivity and response (ego has no place). He is the first person in my life who said $10M isn't a level of money you can get comfortable with. Let me tell you, that shocked me! After meeting him during a mastermind (yes, I paid to get coached yet again), my vision and time horizon changed. I needed to further level up, so I added an aggressive financial target amendment to my contract.

Let's get you from only wanting to get into the room to earning your seat at the table. It is time to address your base understanding of financial literacy and what matters to you. It will help you narrow in on where you need coaching and immediate course correction (or staying the course) and serve as checks and balances to your contract. You may have a vision and quantifiable way to define your success, so let's lay them out right now. The world I am introducing to you requires self-discipline, thirst for knowledge, having your emotions in check, patience, and endurance. Lucky for you, I gave you some points above that will get you thinking and hopefully challenge your views.

As Elon Musk once stated, "If you give yourself 30 days to clean your home, it will take you 30 days. But if you give yourself 3 hours, it will take 3 hours." Our brains are wired to react and respond given the controls and variables in front of us. We have natural biases and for the comfortable "familiar," so we often do not want to spend the extra energy to embark into the "unfamiliar." You will never get to where you want to go without taking the first step. See why I stressed emotional intelligence and human behavior? Everything builds upon each other and takes you from being great to being in the top 1-2%.

Being an Athlete Is a Business

> Take time to think and write out your responses to the questions below to better understand where your financial base state is and what is important to you:

1. What does wealth mean to you?
2. What does "rich" mean to you?
3. What is the difference between rich and wealthy?
4. What is "enough money"? Do you have a number in your head (write it down)?
5. What metric defines your view of what professional and personal success looks like?
6. What is the most important opportunity cost for you?
7. What do you know about legacy building? Do you believe you do this by yourself or with a professional? If with a professional, what does this professional look like pedigree-wise? What can make you build trust faster?
8. Do you believe you can acquire wealth with one job; why?
9. What do you know about a 401K, Roth IRA, or Traditional IRA? What is crypto/ "blockchains"?
10. Currently, how much is your total net worth (everything with value)?
11. Do you believe that you could double and triple that in the short- to medium-term by just making changes? Why or why not?

Refine the above questions every month for two years; I did. It will give you an insight into how you started and where you evolve in terms of wealth and knowledge. You can't hide from yourself, so take this seriously for you. This is just like practice, when no one is watching but the real work gets done. Just know, when I was initially leveling up the bar on my financial literacy and results, I was also in the middle of growing in corporate America (too exhausted to think about anything personally), assessing how to acquire even more success in corporate America (rude awakening we will discuss later), becoming an interim marking director, leading the marketing communication transition spinoff efforts from the $40B company, and starting to negotiate my next role as a global product manager that never existed before. Sheesh, writing and rereading that was exhausting! Long-winded way to say that it takes endurance, discipline, and reframing your mind to become successful and wealthy. I encourage you to challenge and question what you have always known. You may just come away with a breakthrough and lucrative portfolio for generations to come.

The air up top is thin, the waters are murky, and at times, it can be survival of the fittest! I call that another day in paradise to learn and grow! Be excited for the struggle, the wins, and the losses, and "feel all the feels" throughout the journey. Train yourself to handle the changes. Be a chameleon when needed. Be bold when you doubt yourself and want to give up. Remember, we do not stop in the middle of a storm; we power through to the calm after the storm. Align with others well ahead of you. Learn about their journeys, setbacks to comebacks, where they tolerated problems versus failed fast, and how they developed their winning structure. **DO NOT NEGOTIATE WITH YOURSELF! Arm yourself with knowledge and structure.**

Brick by brick, you will get it! Remember, we are just touching the wealth game surface.

I will end this chapter with exactly what I started with, Denzel Washington.

> **Without commitment, you'll never start, but more importantly, without consistency, you'll never finish…. Keep working, keep striving, never give up, fall down 7 times, get up 8. Ease is a greater threat to progress than hardship.**

Success Beyond Game Day Playbook Recap:

Being an Athlete Is a Business: *Use Your Winning Building Blocks Beyond Game Day for Lucrative Outcomes*

1. **Go beyond setting goals** on Day 1. Sign them, and now you have a contract.
    a. Build your structure and don't always think you need to do it alone. Everyone needs a coach and mentorship.
    b. You will need to adapt and be nimble as the world and financial landscape is changing!
    c. If you give yourself one day to complete a task, it will take you one day. But if you give yourself one hour to complete it, then it will take you one hour. Our brains are wired to react and respond given the controls and variables in front of us.

2. **Identify the problem. Do not tolerate problems**, aka red flags.
    a. DO NOT NEGOTIATE WITH YOURSELF! Arm yourself with knowledge and structure.

b. If you can't buy something you want at least 3x that amount, then you walk away. You are not ready (put your ego and pride to the side).

3. **Peel back the layers** and go below the surface. Ask yourself the six whys.
    a. The air up top (high success, executive positions) is thin, and the waters are murky, so be prepared and use the six whys to gain insight to maximize your short windows of opportunity.
    b. "The first million is hard, but the second is inevitable.... It's not becoming a millionaire that's important. It's the person you must become in order to become a millionaire. You have to become a completely different person. You have to develop character beyond 99% of the people in the world. You have to develop honesty and discipline and quality relationships and the willingness and the ability to work and set priorities... because without that, nothing is possible."

4. **Lay the groundwork and foundation** with optionality and flexibility.
    a. Take time to think and write out where your financial base state is and what is important to you. This can get uncomfortable. Deal with it; you can't get to where you want to go without understanding the base.
    b. As you build your championship routine, establishing your financial wealth structure is part of your overall winning strategy. It can serve as your backup and can free you from feeling trapped in a job so you can find a passion you can monetize.

5. **Flawless operationalization.** Game time!
    a. Ease is a greater threat to progress than hardship

11

Higher Highs and Higher Lows

The People and Process Are Your Equalizer

*Believe me, the reward is not so great
without the struggle.*

—Wilma Rudolph

As the great innovator Steve Jobs once said, "If you really look closely, most overnight successes took a long time." We live in a world full of overpromise and underdelivering. Where if you are not first, you are last, even at the expense of quality (which I disagree with). Where you can portray success online but have nothing to your name. Where many companies lead with cost cutting and artificial "growth" reporting to show "higher highs and higher lows," even if that cost cut comes with the devastation of a family during the holidays. If you ask yourself six WHYS, you will always get a better root-cause understanding of someone's thinking and process. Understanding someone's process and why they did what they did to get where they are is more valuable than trying to be "liked enough" or cutting corners to get into the room. I came up with the saying "When you Prepare, Arm, Improvise, and Navigate with an unwavering human-forward approach, you will unlock your true success trajectory." This is my guiding principle and part of my personal value brand proposition (aka I live this daily, and it drives me). Why do you think I waited until the end of the book to throw this concept at you? Let's break it down.

> "When you Prepare, Arm, Improvise, and Navigate with an unwavering human-forward approach, you will unlock your true success trajectory."

Be honest, do you emulate the results of someone successful rather than learn and emulate their journey? I can share how I climbed the ladder from zero years of work experience to leading a +$100M business and worked on multiple complex, career-changing, global projects in between promotions (and raises) while working on generational wealth (leaving money for my kids' kids' kids) in one chapter, but I didn't. **WHY?** It is important for you to see how my journey—leaving no stone unturned, struggling through aspects of growth (physical, mental, and monetarily), feeling exhausted but always moving onward and upward, breaking barriers, and building bridges (like an athlete does)—so YOU can assess and learn from someone who has been down the same road you are embarking on! **WHY?** So you Prepare, Arm, Improvise, and Navigate to streamline (work smarter, not harder) to get to the top by leveraging my learnings for your personal and professional journey! **WHY?** Because I do not want you to be like the many headlines out there stating, "How someone got rich and then lost it all?" but rather see your headline portrayed in the most positive light ever! **WHY?** Because I truly care about helping others and always being human-forward first. **WHY?** If I help you achieve your life success, I believe that you in turn will help that one person who needs you to share your story to kickstart their journey. **WHY?** Because the power of the whole is greater than the parts. All around closing the gap the right way by elevating others. I want to create of community based on opening doors, providing that chance, helping others manage through a potential identity crisis, promote leveraging and connecting, and challenging status quo.

I aspire to leave people better than when I first met them. Six whys later, do you understand where I am taking you? Inspiration is a beautiful thing, and going below the surface level of everything can be your most valuable gift. Care enough to ask the question. Be open-minded to receiving others' perspectives. Create an environment where people matter and their curiosity is welcomed, and reward the behaviors and areas where results were driven by those activities, thus creating a culture.

Let's dig into the meaning of "P" in P.A.I.N. Prepare! You fundamentally know what prepare means and why it is important, but the key question is: Are you prepared for a 20-second quick-win opportunity (think elevator pitch on steroids) just as much as a planned meeting scheduled? You are part of a broader athletic program where you maybe interface with the athletic director (aka CEO of the athletics) and/or senior executives every now and then or in casual passing, right? When you get your "every now and then" interaction, do you utilize the opportunity, or do you fill the air with "hi," "I'm good," "season is great," and "yes/no" answers? Or do you think how you can utilize the proper elevator pitch and capture the senior executives' attention by having them talk about their process and thinking? How did they get to their positions? Do you know? They impact the trajectory of your program that you are building your brand through and leveraging, so why wouldn't you want to know why they make the decisions that they do? Think about that.

One of the major learnings I have had after traveling to over 40 countries is **most people like to talk about themselves** and/or what is inherently comfortable for them, especially if they get to feel good for helping you. It ends up being about them, even when helping you. **Most people are selfish even if they are selfless.** I know that is a tough one to understand, but hear me out. Have you ever thought about why the most affluent people (not all) with money give to charities, major philanthropic endeavors, science grants, scholarships, and/or give free giveaways? They get tax write-offs, which make them more money, and they get to help people, all at the same time. See what I mean? Good intention, but different driving incentive and force. They make more money, and they feel good helping you: a win/win scenario. Think about what we discussed last chapter in terms of value creation with Nike. Own the stock, then buy the shoes, rinse, and repeat! Why have one asset when you can create two and get what you want while creating more value?

Conversely, there are others who genuinely give away and kickstart people's careers because they inherently want to improve the world with one person, breakthrough, and/or solution at a time, but like I mentioned earlier, there are levels to this game! Human behavior gives you a unique opportunity to not only hear what someone is saying but also see and react to different physical, mental, and overall behavioral triggers. Understanding why someone does what they do is multi-faceted and driven by conscious (actively choosing/fully aware) and subconscious (deep-rooted mental compartments that exist, that you may not be aware of) biases. Knowing that people are more than they appear to be and being prepared are your differentiators.

Take a second and think: If you were given a chance to be face-to-face and one-on-one with the athletic director or senior executive, what could you excite, promote, capture, and leverage within 20 seconds? Remember, every day is an interview. Preparation comes from thinking about what you want. Run the six whys in multiple scenarios and line up the information. A lot of work for 20 seconds, right? Think about how many opportunities you have with your Athletic Director (A.D.), MINIMAL. Therefore, your percentage of having to be spot-on and intentional the first time is ever more important. Find the guide that I use to start the process and structure my preparedness below.

Creating More Areas of Intersection

Unprepared ⟶ Intentional

From Random Thoughts Staying Surface Level
"safe, comfortable, easy road, and opportunity costs"

To Finding Intersections Below Surface Level
"proper planning, focused, solidified call to action, and intentional"

- Casual
  - Name and Major
  - How is your practice going?
  - Waits for others to ask questions
- No sense of urgency
- Not situationally aware
- Not mindful of what your opportunity cost is

- Brand Value Proposition: YOU ARE THE BRAND!
  - Who are you?
  - Why do you matter?
  - Where do you want to go?
  - What is important to you?
- Do your homework! Prepare and Arm!
  - Who is the other person? (Professionally and Personally)
  - What is important to them?
  - How can you help them?
  - How can that person help you get where you want to go?
- Find Areas of Intersection: Improvise and Navigate!
  - What is important to you both?
  - Find new connection points throughout the interaction
  - Follow up with a call to action!

You are always one door away from opening a new trajectory of growth. You are one interaction away from extending your network, further translating that to future net worth. And all you need is one yes, one idea, one different perspective to gain momentum. Preparation can help you not only have confidence when the opportunity presents itself but also have a better ability to pivot depending on the conversation. Being able to be nimble and adapt is a trait that very few master. Being prepared will help you drive a conversation around what makes that person excited, what drives them,

> **You are always one door away from opening a new trajectory of growth.**

why they make the decisions they do, their management style, and/or their overall cues they give off for you to rapidly leverage and take a conversation from 20 seconds to being invited to lunch because you hit the right string. **Proper Planning Prevents Piss Poor Performance!**

Now that you are prepared (or will be), let's take you to the "A" in P.A.I.N. Arm Yourself! This one is the hardest, in my opinion. When you are prepared and you know your work ethic (an athlete differentiator), you may fall into the "I know how to do it right the first time" and "I can do it faster versus handing it off to others" trap. **Why?** Because you are an athlete, and we always step up. **Why?** If you have another person helping, it will inherently slow everything down because you must explain. **Why?** Because you have a certain level of work quality that you expect from yourself every time. **Why?** Because that one time you didn't have it perfect or someone else messed it up, you got into a situation that caused you a certain reactivity and response you did not enjoy. **Why?** Because you tried to test the new waters in an area, you felt you were the expert or had decent experience in, and you couldn't control the outcome. **Why?** Because you are an athlete, you know how to win, no one tells you what you can and can't do, and failure is not an option.

If this resonates with you, just know, it is a normal feeling. I was always the one who controlled projects, tagged the "worker bee," and somehow, I was proud of that. If you are this person, pause for a second and stop what you are doing. In business, they love to use people like us. Corporate America will eat this up and use every bit of the "urgency to get things done," "orientation toward results," and "unwavering tenacity" you bring to the table. Just know if you keep delivering a Lambo when all they asked for was a Honda, why would they ever need to give you a raise or promotion? You already give them high quality and go above and beyond for your pay grade. Why would they promote you? You have a boss or team who is terrified to lose you now because you are doing everyone else's jobs. I am not saying manage expectations to a bare minimum output; be you, but be mindful if you are not taking others along for the ride and of the implications that can cause.

Conversely, you may be the one doing the bare minimum in your classes or anything outside of your current sports. **Why?** Because you see others stepping up and wanting to run the show, and that works for you. You must step up all the time in your sport, so it's a "nice break." **Why?** Because you are exhausted by always putting in 150% based on your assessment and the eagerness of those around you trying to impress you. You are good with the product they will deliver. **Why?** It is a lot easier to manage from the sidelines, and then you can keep your focus on your sport. **Why?** Because you are at a point in your career where people know you, want to go above and beyond for you because you play a sport and are on TV. You think, why not leverage your status for an easy A. **Why?** You really do not know the topic or class curriculum because you haven't spent the time learning. If it isn't about your sport or what it will take to get to the higher elite sports level, then you do not see the ROI (return on investment). **Why?** You ultimately want to keep up the façade of your athletic avatar that is "top elite, cool athlete who is slated to make a ton of money in pro," but deep down, you are afraid to be vulnerable and fail outside of sports. Failure in an arena outside of your popular place of comfort, an uncharted territory that may lead to people's perceptions of you changing versus the "god-like complex" they place on you now.

If this resonates with you directly and/or indirectly, I get it! There are many people in the world who do this across the globe in business. Just know, when the lights go down (everyone retires), or if you are hurt from that sport that you put all your eggs in the basket for, the setback for the comeback will be tough. Just know they love you when the lights are on, but when the lights turn off in the stadium, how many of those fans will truly be there for you? You are more than your sport, so challenge yourself to be bigger than the persona and façade of being an athlete. Truly start to understand that being an athlete is a business and failing is a part of the game. It takes one door to open, so you must be consistent. Build your stock value every day with your team in sports, school, business, and life. Be ready. Be multi-faceted, not singular in your approach.

Arming yourself with the people and tools you need is paramount. Be ambitious and remember that sometimes there is no "I" in team. Conversely, sometimes there is a perfect place to tap into the notion that there is a "M" and an "E" in team. Be one of the whole, but know you cannot be good for the whole until you are good for you. This intentional focus on you applies to business, sports, relationships, and life in general.

The same applies for the family members in your life or "Day 1s" who may require more than you can give at the current moment. There will be a lot of people who want things from you as an athlete, so being prepared and armed with the people and process can differentiate what success looks like for you. What will be tough here is you may need to leave behind some people. You may have to say NO to your family and friends at times, and just know that is required to draw the line in the sand. **If it isn't about your mission, part of the purpose behind "you the brand," and tied to your (goal) contract, then it must go. Arming yourself is humbling and tough because you must let go of some comfortable dead weight while reconciling if someone else is more equipped to help versus you doing it yourself. Once you do this, your world changes.** It is very rare that the highest level of success can be achieved by one person. You need the right team, working on the right ideas and solutions at the right time with all the right tools. This has been my business eureka.

Once you prepare thoroughly and arm yourself with the right people and process, the fun comes when things do not go as planned. My favorite in P.A.I.N. is "I" for improvise. **Being able to improvise takes practice (and a lot of failed attempts). It is not just about winging it, but rather about being prepared and armed so you can change the outcome while in the gray area.** Those who are willing to fail fast, learn, take another step, and fail again to take another step are the real winners in my mind.

I know it is easy to say that it takes "one yes" and "one door" to change your trajectory but listen to me clearly: With improvising, you learn how to change outcomes based on real-time pivoting. As an athlete, the "I" should feel most comfortable, and at times, you typically will be your saving grace when you don't come as prepared as you would like. When you tap into the muscle memory that you acquired through trial and error through your athletic career, you become THE changemaker! This is where I further differentiated myself from others in corporate America. Be the starter and the bullpen!

With improvising, you learn how to change outcomes based on real-time pivoting.

How powerful would you feel if you were able to take an uncontrollable situation and turn it into intentional and actionable opportunities at the flip of a switch? And we have arrived at the **"N" in P.A.I.N. Navigate! Steer the boat! Drive the championship routine. Navigation is the compass requirement needed to get the results. Triangulation point to point. It helps guide your call to action!**

Imagine you are in the middle of a game; someone gets hurt, and in real time you get put in a position that you have never practiced before. Or think of a time when you were playing your sport, your whole playbook based on film and scouting reports, and then suddenly you were faced with a completely different scheme or system from the other side. You may get yourself handed a rude awakening in the first couple of plays, but then you improvise, reset, forget the playbook for a second, and know you are prepared for this, you practiced, and you armed yourself with the right tools alongside your team. You improvise and proceed to find a way to navigate the game to a "W" by leveraging your learnings from your well-established athletic career and unwavering drive. You are more than an athlete; you are a force to be reckoned with! You are built to handle when the limelight is on you, and you know the real championship routines get built while you work in silence. You have a bandwidth many aspire to have but very few achieve. You are the denominator when it comes to navigating toward the 'ship!

You will begin to learn what the switch looks and feels like while training yourself how to turn it on and off on demand. You are armed with the skills and toolbox acquired over those years, so it is critical you trust in your ability to get the job done. You improvise when you don't have the right tools in place and must adapt. And you will always find a way to navigate to the successful outcome, even if you are scared or in uncharted territories, because you are an athlete, and you know how to win! You always find a way to flawlessly triangulate all situations ahead. These traits are in our athlete DNA.

Do you think your coach will look at that "one-time fluke" or notice if you didn't do everything perfect, despite the win? A win is a win is a win! It doesn't always have to be pretty. Your coaches and teammates will have a newfound respect for your ability to step up and be the changemaker. There is where the "there is no 'I' in team" harmoniously jives with "but there is a 'M' and 'E' in team." Perfect mix of you versus you, and for the greater good of the team. Doesn't get much better than that!

Displaying your grit and character in the thick of the heat and pressure—this is where the diamond (YOU) forms! **From my experience, the most beautiful things in life come from being vulnerable and going below the surface. This is where you need to go every chance you get to ultimately go where you need to go, "your sixth why".** Feel all the feels and walk through the murky waters to areas of ambiguity. The walk will not be for the faint at heart, but when embraced will lead to major breakthroughs. As an athlete, dealing with the unknown and producing a "W" is well within your wheelhouse.

Going back to that 20-second conversation with your AD or senior executive. Leveraging my structure above can prepare you with the critical details that many do not spend the time to think through. Understanding what is important to a person professionally and personally will always arm you better and help you improvise when needed. It is important to be agile when you learn something new, especially when you are operating in that small window.

Structure can help guide you with a framework (aka playbook) that can be utilized over and over. It is important to not be obsessively confined to operate within this structure because if you do, you may miss many doors with insane opportunities, or in some cases, this could slow down your true success trajectory. Truly understanding people and leveraging processes have been two key areas that enabled me to find the most important doors that led to major seats at the table. The mentality and game can shift by just changing your headspace

The mentality and game can shift by just changing your headspace and going below the surface to find the most missed, most discrete details.

and going below the surface to find the most missed, most discrete details.

You already know how to sacrifice, be self-disciplined, and build a championship routine, but now, all I am helping you do is to endure P.A.I.N. in many ways so your toolbox is equipped with what you need, when you need it. You should know, when an athlete puts their mind to something, it gets done. Even if you fail the first time, your obsessive focus, consistency, and drive to be the best and aspire to perform at the highest caliber is why I know you can be better than me. That is what we do as athletes: We inspire, embrace the mundane consistency required daily, drive that inner beast mode to compete, raise the bar, and keep chasing the dream. **The only difference now is I am raising your "dream" to a contract with timelines for yourself. Consider me your accountability partner. You versus you, but you better be ready to compete, because I am coming for you.**

12

Raise the Bar: Elevation Requires Separation

Start Before You Are Ready

> *Excellence is not a singular act but a habit.*
> *You are what you repeatedly do.*
>
> —Shaquille O'Neal

One day, you will near the end of that stellar high school, college, or pro sports career. Are you emotionally prepared for that? Does it give you anxiety to know that your next step may have nothing to do with sports? How does that make you feel? Who do you see around you when the limelight is not on you? Oh, that day will come sooner than you can imagine. Even Tom Brady has finally retired. It's part of the game. So, guess what? YOU get to build a new championship routine!

I understand what it feels like to lose your identity post-sports, an identity that you spent your whole life building. Remember, never stop during the heart of the storm. It too shall pass. Tap into your network and leverage your mentors. You do not have to embark on this alone. On the other side of every struggle is a broader reason why you had to "grow through what you go through." I made it to the other side (just like you will) and felt reborn (in a way) when I started to scale the ladder as a corporate trailblazer.

I worked hard to get there, I built structures on how to leverage my athletic skills in corporate settings (hint, hint—basis of the book), and I led by building bridges and garnering relationships that were rooted in genuine care. I know what it feels like to build a career from zero years of experience, create my own identity and roles from a white sheet of paper, become part of the leadership track, travel to over 40 countries, then have to restart with a spinoff business and grow multiple businesses within the spinoff to become multimillion growth engines and then decide to leave it all behind for my life's passion, all by the wee age of 34 years old. Yes, the anxiety starts to pour through my veins, my body gets hot, my heart beats a million miles a minute every time I think about leaving a lucrative six-figure career (that I still have fun doing) to start my own business. Helping athletes like you around the globe succeed beyond game day by utilizing their athlete advantage is MY SIXTH WHY!

You are probably thinking, sheesh, there is a lot in this book. What are the three or four key takeaways? (Thank you, I'm glad you asked!)

1. **Feel all the feels and live with the P.A.I.N. (Prepare, Arm, Improvise, Navigate).**

2. **Fail often and fail fast; do not tolerate problems (even if that problem is a person).**

3. **Go below surface level and utilize the "six whys" to help you get there.**

4. **Start before you are ready; manage your reactivity and response.**

When you think about feeling all the feels and living with the P.A.I.N., just know this takes practice and discipline. **How you do anything is how you do everything!** There is a lot of work done at the front end to prepare you to be ready when that door opens on the back end. Think of this as that mundane athletic schedule you are used to doing already, the amount of practice and film you watch for the few hours you play that opponent in a game/match. You know how to do the work when no one is watching. Sometimes you don't get to pick the time the door presents itself, but you can control your intention and focus on how to prepare ahead of it—more proactive, less reactive.

> **How you do anything is how you do everything!**

We have discussed arming yourself with the skills and/or team needed. Building a championship routine means you need to get others on the train to help you on your journey. Doing this frees you up to focus on the critical aspects and gives you more time to spend on your highest quality output and return on investment. Building the RIGHT TEAM of experts results in the highest quality and faster success. **This is not a "get rich tomorrow" program; this is a "go through the journey and put the right things in the right place and let it marinate (requires major patience and discipline)" mindset.**

I challenge you to take it a step further and think about unarming yourself from others who don't fit your purpose. The word "fire" is harsh, but I want you to understand that I (and many others) can look at who you hang with and learn a lot about you. Your network is your net worth. Hear me clearly here: Elevation requires separation. If you do not have people around you who are striving to better themselves and raising the bar, you will be forced to come down to their level versus having them meet you up top. If you don't align with the right people, you are essentially tolerating a problem, which will result in constant failure (like a hamster wheel)! You need to lose the dead weight. **Do not give up on people, but realize that you cannot make others want what you want. It is tough, but it is a necessary evil.**

I asked you above, when the limelight is gone, who will be around you? If you had five to 10 people, including family, I would be impressed. Your inner circle will get smaller as you grow. I know you do not get to pick your family, but this goes for anyone in your life. If you have others leeching off you, you will always be held back because they will take too much of your energy. Help others who are working to get there and keep those gems who are behind you but actively structure themselves to meet you there! They are working to raise the bar and close the gap in the right way. Best way to visualize this is playing down to competition and losing the game when you know you should have won. Stick to the plan, stay consistent, always be disciplined, and play your game!

You will be an emotional roller coaster through this process, so feel all the highs and lows. You will learn so much, and that beast mode switch will carry you through the murky waters. YOU ARE BUILT FOR THIS! Commit 100% and trust the process. You know how to think on your feet, so improvising is an area where you, the athlete, shines. Imagine when you are thoroughly prepared and have already thought about most of the scenarios and mapped out the outcomes/calls to action. You go from

> **YOU ARE BUILT FOR THIS! Commit 100% and trust the process.**

rookie to expert real quick! You know how to win. Ever think why many people across the world use sports analogies?

Sports are the common global language, where everyone can speak the same language! Not everyone in the world speaks English, and that is known as the "common language." But if you throw a ball around or kick an object between two milk cartons in any part of the world, **there is an equal footing and understanding despite language barriers.**

If many people and specifically corporations around the world use sports analogies to excite, incentivize, and drive their teams, don't you think you have a leg up on others? You have lived through what most "talk" through. You grew through what you went through. No talk. Straight real-world experience. You know the actual feeling of making that big play, winning or losing in the playoffs, and the everyday grind you must endure to be ready for that next game. **You are the advantage in every situation. You are a part of the select few that can say they have done it.** Now do you understand the title of the book? You are the advantage. **This has nothing to do with me and everything to do with your athlete advantage to succeed beyond game day.**

As you move toward life after your sports career, just think one step at a time, and when you feel the weight of the world on you, keep pushing. Do not ease up! Ease is your greatest threat. Do not stop working out; do not stop your routine. I did that and let my health take a back seat for far too long! Do not hide behind anything. Own everything you do 100%. Learn from it, fail fast, and more importantly, **FAIL OFTEN.** When you fail (everyone does), you will need to take the lessons, implement them immediately, and most importantly, prevent the repeat of the same problem. This is a straight rinse and repeat, exactly like Grandma's advice.

I have now gotten to a point in my life where I aim for failure in everything I do personally and professionally. I want to see where my boundaries are at all times. What I have learned is as the bar goes up, I soar higher, and my lows are higher than before. Raising the bar takes intention and drive every day, just like you would do in the weight room or in practice. Once you get past the idea of "not being right" and shift your mentality to "learn, leverage, and level up," you will see changes in how you approach the former unapproachable problems. You go from not wanting to deal with problems to hitting them straight on! You go from the one in the group solving all of the problems to the leader orchestrating the whole team dynamic! This concept applies to all facets of your professional and personal growth.

When your championship routine is in place, just know, you will need to go below the surface to truly go where you want to go. Even if you do not aspire to be an executive, but rather a blue-collar craftsman, you will still need to build teams, understand your customers, and connect with people. Understanding what drives people is one of the lowest-hanging fruits out there. People wanted their efforts valued and heard. People matter, so build continuous bridges. I do not care how mean or rude someone is, always try to fund the six whys. You may be a solution to their problem, so take it on yourself to go the extra mile.

Spend the time early and often with your team. When you think you have it figured it out, take them out to lunch and continue to learn more. People change and evolve, just like you are doing now, so as you continuously improve your approach professionally (and personally), don't you think you need to have empathy and lead with emotional intelligence? In your job, you will spend hours upon hours with your team. In many cases, they become your dysfunctional work family. Treat this with the respect it deserves.

Ask six whys before you ever rationalize, assume, or improvise. Trust but verify when needed, but enable others to make decisions. It is okay to fail across the board. Don't always solve everyone else's problems to avoid "rework." Join them on their journey, but let them go through what they go through. Help shepherd them from going off the rail track. Be upfront with others and come prepared with how best to interact with them. If you don't handle issues when the air gets thin, you could turn your best asset, person, or team into a tolerated problem, which could turn into a liability. Be careful here! Deal with it!

And my favorite, my bread and butter, is **START BEFORE YOU ARE READY**! If you wait to have everything lined out and perfect, you may prevent something fantastic from coming into the picture. As I progressed my career at lightning speed, I said yes to all the opportunities and found ways to deliver the highest quality results. Sometimes I actually led the charge, but other times, I had to motivate others who had the skill sets I did not have to get where we needed to go. On "paper" I had never managed anyone before, but hold up, I was the captain of an NCAA softball team. I helped lead the charge but needed to rely on the team to do their part just as much as I would. I call that experience if I ever knew it! You have what you need to get the job done, so start before you are ready!

START BEFORE YOU ARE READY!

Half the battle is going into the unknown and managing your reactivity and response. When you have your "off day," it is just a bad day, not a bad life! If you let situations drive how you feel to the core, then you need a reset. Walk away, go work out, get a bite to eat, or call someone and tell them how much you appreciate them. This life will feel heavy at times, but, hey, do the best you can within your means, and I promise it will eventually work itself out.

Success Beyond Game Day

It is a funny thing when you are in the middle of a situation and you are convinced that it is the hardest, most difficult, and never-ending time in the current moment. Now think about an actual time in high school where you had a tough test or were studying for finals, and then compare that to college finals. What about when you were in middle school playing ball, versus playing in college while the world watched? After all of that, then you graduated, and now post-sports is your new tough, aka "impossible." You look back and think, sheesh, I had it easy in middle school, high school, and so on. Your mental mindset can shift a bad day to a good one. **Mind over matter is still my motto when I take on challenging assignments and/or personal situations going on.**

Look at me now. I started the process before I was ready, while still working full-time in corporate America, filming on my "days off," mentoring many athletes (formally and informally) during my lunch breaks because I found my life's purpose. My goal is not just to write a book. My mission is so much bigger than that, and I am hopeful you know that by now.

I genuinely want to provide a safe space for you to learn freely, leverage your athlete advantage, and ask all the questions you may have but you never ask out in the open. I aim to prepare you for all the opportunities ahead and help you build your structure, find ways to arm you with information, show you how to improvise by leveraging your game day antics, and get you the access you need to walk through that open door and take a seat at the table. I want you to practice with me, so when the time comes, you will own every room you walk in by being 100% yourself. I look forward to partnering with you so you can leverage what I have done to get where I am today and then in turn, be better than I ever could be! I have been where you are, and I am here to show you there is light at the end of the tunnel. I must ask you one more time, who are you outside of sports? (You better have this nailed down by now!)

I see a future shaper and leader in you who is more than equipped to pave the way. The journey can be scary, but you are an athlete; you know how to win. When you utilize my guiding playbook, you will see how the game can slow down for you. You will see the full field of play to make your next move. This is not an end-all, be-all playbook. This is the start to helping you set your initial structure up for your legacy success. Only you can determine what your guiding principles are, so learn from others, take the sauce that works, and make it your own!

This is more than the game. This is about your brand, your journey, and your life! How you do anything is how you do everything. Being an athlete and performing on the biggest stages gives you the leg up on everyone else who hasn't had the privilege. The sacrifices and experiences we grow through do not end when you win that championship or big game but rather become solidified building blocks for all of your future life's success. I went from zero years of work experience to leading a +$100M business line. I didn't have what you "should" have on paper to be a part of a team and help drive a $10B merger and acquisition project in five weeks, but I got in the room, learned from others who were elite, and left my impact out on the field.

> *Character cannot be developed in ease and quiet. Only through experience of trial and suffering can the soul be strengthened, ambition inspired, and success achieved.*
>
> —Helen Keller

I own being a master at failing fast. I own that with the right preparation, team, and structure in place you can be

as ambitious and successful as you want to be. I am not confined to process, but I utilize what works and continuously improve as I go. This is not a static journey, so be prepared to tweak and modify as you go! I can always set up for the repeat championship win because I am the Athlete Advantage with a toolbox full of versatile options. I choose to build my brand on being an athlete for a lifetime forward. Will you?

Endnotes

1. Dalio, Ray. *Principles: Life and Work.* Simon & Schuster, 2017.
2. Robbins, Steve L. *What If?: Short Stories to Spark Diversity Dialogue.* Nicholas Brealey, 2018.
3. Robbins, Steve L. *What If?: Short Stories to Spark Diversity Dialogue.* Nicholas Brealey, 2018.
4. Source: https://academy.binance.com/en/articles/what-makes-a-blockchain-secure

About the Author

Samantha Card is a former NCAA Division 1 athlete, MBA graduate, bestselling author, Fortune 100 company trailblazer, and "level up" expert. She didn't grow up with traditional work experience because she played year-round, excelling on the field and becoming one of the top 5% of competitive athletes to play in Division 1 sports. After graduating with a Bachelor of Science degree in Chemistry, she experienced a full-blown identity crisis. "Who am I outside of sports?"

Recovering from high-functioning anxiety that followed the transition beyond the game, Samantha "grew through what she went through" despite the outside world thinking she had it all together. Samantha tapped into her athletic building blocks, reestablished a routine, and found ways to leverage her sports vehicle by repackaging the experiential skill sets she amassed through her athletic career. She graduated with an MBA from the University of Pittsburgh Katz School of Business.

In 2022, Samantha left her corporate career to pursue her unwavering global mission to help inspire, empower, and support athletes, coaches, administrators, active military, veterans, and corporate athletes to extend their skills and impact beyond their roles. She brings out the high-performance mindset in

About the Author

others and prepares them to GO Pro In Life by identifying opportunities, taking swift action, failing fast often, and applying an ALL-IN mindset. She currently lives in Florida.

Connect with Samantha at SuccessBeyondGameday.com

THIS BOOK IS PROTECTED INTELLECTUAL PROPERTY

The author of this book values Intellectual Property. The book you just read is protected by Easy IP™, a proprietary process, which integrates blockchain technology giving Intellectual Property "Global Protection." By creating a "Time-Stamped" smart contract that can never be tampered with or changed, we establish "First Use" that tracks back to the author.

Easy IP™ functions much like a Pre-Patent™ since it provides an immutable "First Use" of the Intellectual Property. This is achieved through our proprietary process of leveraging blockchain technology and smart contracts. As a result, proving "First Use" is simple through a global and verifiable smart contract. By protecting intellectual property with blockchain technology and smart contracts, we establish a "First to File" event.

Powered By Easy IP™

LEARN MORE AT EASYIP.TODAY

www.ingramcontent.com/pod-product-compliance
Lightning Source LLC
Chambersburg PA
CBHW051828160426
43209CB00040B/1981/J